Reader's Digest
Pathfinders

Insects and Spiders

A Reader's Digest Pathfinder

Reader's Digest Children's Books are published by
Reader's Digest Children's Publishing, Inc.
Reader's Digest Road, Pleasantville, NY, 10570-7000, U.S.A.

Conceived and produced by Weldon Owen Pty Limited
59 Victoria Street, McMahons Point, NSW, 2060, Australia
A member of the Weldon Owen Group of Companies
Sydney • San Francisco • Auckland • London

© 2000 Weldon Owen Inc.

READER'S DIGEST CHILDREN'S PUBLISHING, INC.
Senior Project Editors: Sherry Gerstein, Beverly Larson
Associate Editor: Dina Rubin
Assistant Editor: Lori Froeb
Project Creative Director: Candy Warren
Art Director: Fredric Winkowski
Production Coordinator: Debbie Gagnon
Director of Sales and Marketing: Rosanne McManus

WELDON OWEN PUBLISHING
Chief Executive Officer: John Owen
President: Terry Newell
Publisher: Sheena Coupe
Associate Publisher: Lynn Humphries
Art Director: Sue Burk
Consultant, Design Concept and Cover Design: John Bull
Design Concept: Clare Forte, Robyn Latimer
Editorial Assistants: Sarah Anderson, Tracey Jackson
Production Manager: Caroline Webber
Vice President International Sales: Stuart Laurence

Author: Matthew Robertson
Consultants: Louis N. Sorkin, B.C.E.; Dr. David Grimaldi
Project Editor: Bronwyn Sweeney
Designer: Ivan Finnegan
Picture Research: Annette Crueger

Illustrators: Sandra Doyle/Wildlife Art Ltd, Christer Eriksson, Ray Grinaway,
Ian Jackson/Wildlife Art Ltd, James McKinnon, Rob Mancini,
Steve Roberts/Wildlife Art Ltd, Chris Shields/Wildlife Art Ltd, Kevin Stead

Library of Congress Cataloging–in–Publication Data

Robertson, Matthew.
Insects and spiders / [Matthew Robertson].
p.   cm. — (Reader's Digest pathfinders)
Summary: Uses text, illustrations, and activities to present all sorts of information about insects and spiders.
ISBN 1-57584-375-7 (hc.: alk. paper). — ISBN 1-57584-381-1 (lib. ed. : alk. paper) —
ISBN 1-57584-983-6 (trade paperback edition)
1. Insects Juvenile literature. 2. Spiders Juvenile literature.
[1. Insects. 2. Spiders.] I. Title. II. Series.
QL467.2.R64 2000   595.7—d   c21 99-36390

Color Reproduction by Colourscan Co Pte Ltd
Printed by Tien Wah Press Pte Ltd
Printed in Singapore

A WELDON OWEN PRODUCTION

Reader's Digest
Pathfinders

Insects and Spiders

Reader's
Digest
Children's Books™

Pleasantville, New York • Montréal, Québec

Contents

Pick Your Path!

THE WORLD IS TEEMING with animals—some of which live no farther than your backyard or even your own home. Are you ready to learn more about life on the wing? Open the pages of *Insects and Spiders* and prepare to be amazed. Read straight through to find out about insects and spiders from the inside out. Or try something different. Have you always wanted to know more about the "hive mentality"? Sneak a peek at the real thing in "Stings on Wings" and read on from there.

You'll find plenty of other discovery paths to choose from in the special features sections. Get insight into insect and spider behavior in "Inside Story," or meet nature head-on with "Hands On" activities.

INSIDE STORY
World in Miniature

Watch a smart spider at work. Learn from experts who've used one insect to control the population of another. Read more about that summertime scourge, the menacing mosquito. Then look out—a pack of driver ants is ready to hit town! With INSIDE STORY, you'll get an insider's look at the way insects and spiders have affected the world around us. You'll never look at an anthill or a spiderweb in the same way again.

HANDS ON
Create and Make

Use paper and a spoonful of jam to test ants' food-finding faculties. Learn the best techniques for locating and caring for insects. Search your surroundings for cicadas. Find out where to look for your local spiders. The HANDS ON features offer experiments, projects, and activities that will bring the world of insects and spiders to life.

Word Builders

What a strange word! What does it mean? Where did it come from? Find out by reading *Word Builders*.

That's Amazing!

Awesome facts, amazing records, fascinating figures— you'll find them all in *That's Amazing!*

Pathfinder

Use the *Pathfinder* section to find your way from one subject to another. It's all up to you.

Ready! Set!
Start exploring!

Introducing... Insects

GET READY TO meet some of Earth's smallest inhabitants. Learn how insects work from the inside out—how they live, communicate, change, and grow. Then get acquainted with some of the stars of the insect world. Find out what it takes to be a true bug. After that, meet the beetles—the most numerous insects of all. Admire delicate butterflies and moths, and then go underground with a colony of ants. Take a look inside a beehive before zooming off with the flies. It's time to meet nature head-on. Just turn the page.

Spider

Tick

Millipede

Scorpion

What Is an Insect?

FACT: INSECTS ARE the most successful animals on Earth. Think about it. Scientists have already identified more than 1 million different insect species, but there might be as many as 30 million out there. And some of those species have been around for millions of years, too.

Insects belong to a group of animals called arthropods, which also includes spiders, scorpions, crabs, and millipedes. One thing that all these creatures have in common is that they have a tough outer shell instead of an internal skeleton. The shell, known as an exoskeleton, is made from a material called chitin. This substance is remarkably light, yet it's as strong as steel. The result is a protective outer coat that doesn't weigh its owner down.

Each subgroup of arthropods has its own unique characteristics. Insects, in particular, have bodies that are usually divided into three parts. The first part is the head, which has the eyes, two antennae, the mouthparts, and the brain. The second section is the thorax, to which the wings and three pairs of legs are attached. It also holds all the muscles that work these legs and wings. Last is the abdomen, containing the rest of the insect's internal organs. Most insects—from a butterfly to a cockroach—have these features in common.

ALL IN THE FAMILY

Crabs, spiders, scorpions, millipedes, centipedes, ticks, and mites are all arthropods. Each group differs from insects in various ways. For instance, some have eight legs, like scorpions and spiders. Others, like millipedes, have bodies that are made up of many more than three main parts.

Thorax
The legs and wings are attached to the thorax.

Head
The head is one of the strongest body parts—good protection for the brain.

Antennae
With these two sense organs, an insect can detect chemicals, heat, and vibrations.

Compound eye
Each of the tiger beetle's compound eyes has 26,000 lenses packed together.

Palps
These sense organs are used to taste food and help guide it into the mouth.

Mandibles
In this insect, the jaws are tough, sharp, and powered by strong muscles.

HANDS ON

Bug Safari

Wherever you live, there are bound to be insects nearby. It's just that they aren't always easy to see. A good way to meet some of your insect neighbors is to lay a white sheet under a low branch of a tree or shrub. Make sure there are no wasps' nests, then rap the branch a few times with a stick. Any insects on the branch will be knocked onto the sheet. If you try different kinds of trees, you will find different types of insects. Once you have finished looking at the insects, put them back at the base of the tree. You can use the same sheet to make a light trap to attract night fliers. Hang the sheet up outside, on a clothesline or over a balcony, and turn on a strong flashlight behind it. Wait and see what insects fly your way.

Butterfly

Thrips

Word Builders

• An **arthropod** has jointed legs and an external skeleton. The word is from the ancient Greek words *arthron*, for "joint," and *podos*, for "foot."
• **Exoskeleton** comes from the ancient Greek: *exo*, meaning "outside," and *skeletos*, meaning "dried up, hard." An insect's skeleton is on the outside. It is made up of plates joined together by more flexible membranes, which let the insect bend and twist.

That's Amazing!

• Some insects live in very harsh habitats and conditions. The petroleum fly lives in puddles of crude oil. It feeds on insects that fall in and get stuck.
• Snow fleas can survive in subzero temperatures. But if you pick one up, the heat from your hand will kill it in seconds.
• The larvae of some midges can be put in boiling water and still survive.

Path

• To mee
turn to pages 2
• Beetles have e
have specialized wing
• Discover the differe
spiders and insects on pages 48–49.

A Tiger on Six Legs

With its large eyes, razor-sharp jaws, and powerful running legs, this beautiful tiger beetle deserves its name. It is a true predator. Its eyes are able to detect the smallest movements of a potential victim. Its legs can carry it along at speeds that outrun most other insects— either to catch them or avoid being caught by them.

Elytra and wings
A beetle has elytra, or wing cases. They protect the delicate flying wings beneath.

Abdomen
Usually the largest part of an insect's body, the abdomen contains most of the vital organs.

Leg
Most insects have six legs. The legs vary in length and are usually divided into five parts.

Foot
An insect's feet may have hooks, pads, or suckers to help it hold on to surfaces or food.

Trapped in Time

Fossils of insects date back 400 million years. Insect remains are very fragile, so not much survives to become fossils. Sometimes, though, creatures like this 40-million-year-old grasshopper were trapped in the sticky sap of trees. When the sap fossilized and turned into amber, the grasshopper was perfectly preserved.

Silverfish   *Lacewing*

The Success Story

Insects occur in almost all the world's habitats, including oceans, polar zones, and mountain peaks. The animals below are all crickets, but each has made adaptations to its individual surroundings.

Green Can't Be Seen

Living in forests and grasslands, a great green bush cricket needs good camouflage to avoid predators. Large eyes scan for danger, while long legs and wings help with a quick getaway.

Field Work

The field cricket has strong, multipurpose mouthparts to deal with its varied diet. Its long and powerful back legs help it to hop or push its way through the grass of the meadows where it lives.

Digging the Dirt

The Jerusalem cricket spends most of its life below ground. It has stout, powerful legs for digging. Wings might get in the way, so it has none.

Up Close and Personal

INSECTS HAVE THE SAME basic bodily functions we have—they eat, breathe, move, and have babies. The difference is in how it all happens. Insect blood carries nutrients to body parts and removes wastes just like human blood, but is pumped by a long, thin heart that stretches through the abdomen. Insect blood is yellow or green because it contains certain proteins.

Another difference is that insects have no lungs. Instead, they get oxygen through openings along the sides of their bodies called spiracles. Spiracles are connected to tracheae, which branch out into smaller tubes that carry oxygen to every part of the insect. Functions like this are controlled by the large brain, which is connected to all nerves by a long nerve cord.

To keep all these systems running, an insect needs energy from food. In the case of this wasp (right), the food is mixed with saliva in the mouth. It passes down the throat to the crop, where it is broken down by more saliva and other secretions. Then it heads for the stomach, where special enzymes churn up the food further, making it ready for the insect to use.

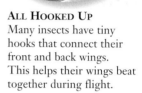

ALL HOOKED UP
Many insects have tiny hooks that connect their front and back wings. This helps their wings beat together during flight.

INSIDE OUT
With its external skeleton cut away, this wasp's organs are revealed in color code. The breathing system is light blue. The system for digesting food is green. The blood circulation system is red, and the central nervous system is dark blue.

INSIDE STORY

Taking Insect Pics

Insects are small, and that makes it hard to photograph them. The solution: Put a magnifying glass on the camera! With a special macro lens, an insect can be magnified several times. Attach a microscope to a camera, and you can magnify an insect hundreds of times. But the most powerful way to magnify insects is with a scanning electron microscope. The resulting image, called an electron micrograph, isn't really a normal photo at all. It is a computer-generated image created by bouncing electrons off an object so that they strike a sensor. With this machine, it's possible to magnify an insect 20,000 times its normal size, like this picture of a fly.

Heart
An insect has no arteries or veins. The tubelike heart pumps blood around the body.

Air sac
These pocketlike sacs allow the insect to store oxygen.

Ventral nerve cord
This connects series of nerve bundles, or ganglia, which help control many organs.

Stomach
Food goes through its final digestion stage in the stomach.

A THING CALLED STING
The barbed stinger of a honeybee is shown here, threaded through the eye of a needle. When used, the barbs get stuck, causing a deadly injury to the bee when it tries to crawl away. Wasps have smooth stingers that can be used many times.

Spiracle
Insects usually have between 2 and 11 pairs of air holes.

Ant

Ladybug

• **Trachea** comes from the Latin word *trachia*, for "windpipe." Tracheae are thin tubes that carry oxygen to every cell in an insect's body, and waste gases, such as carbon dioxide, out of the body.

• **Ganglia** are clusters of nerve cells that act as control centers. An insect has ganglia along its nerve cord, and its brain is made up of three ganglia which contain thousands of nerve cells.

• Some wasps lay eggs in other creatures. Find out why on page 16.
• Insects are eating machines. Learn what foods drive these machines on pages 32–35.
• What insects have the most painful sting? Go to page 43.

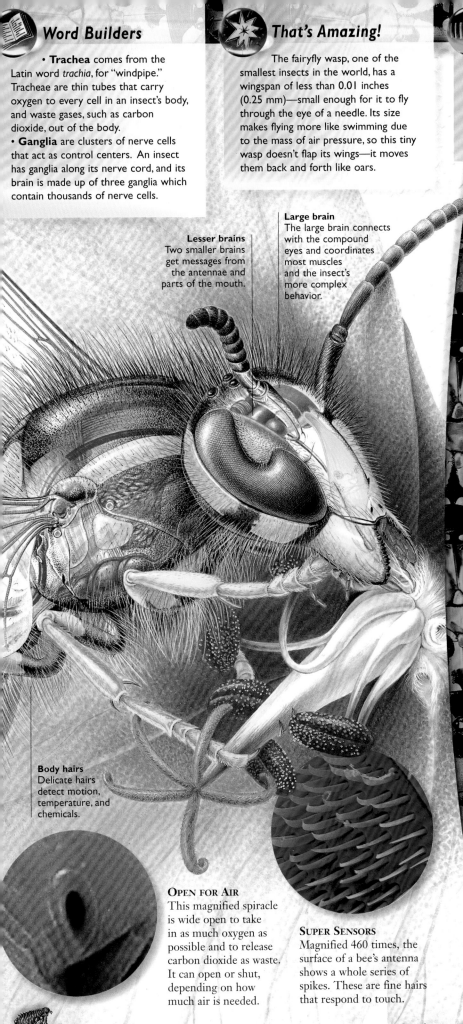

Lesser brains
Two smaller brains get messages from the antennae and parts of the mouth.

Large brain
The large brain connects with the compound eyes and coordinates most muscles and the insect's more complex behavior.

Body hairs
Delicate hairs detect motion, temperature, and chemicals.

OPEN FOR AIR
This magnified spiracle is wide open to take in as much oxygen as possible and to release carbon dioxide as waste. It can open or shut, depending on how much air is needed.

SUPER SENSORS
Magnified 460 times, the surface of a bee's antenna shows a whole series of spikes. These are fine hairs that respond to touch.

Flea

Grasshopper

BREATH OF AIR

AIR HOLES
Most insects take in air through spiracles on the sides of their thorax and abdomen. Spiracles are often hard to see, but they are quite visible on this tobacco hornworm caterpillar.

SNORKELS
Insects that live underwater still need to breathe air. Some mosquito larvae pierce the surface of the water with a snorkel-like breathing tube that sticks up from the tip of their abdomen.

AIR BUBBLES
To make sure it has an air supply when swimming underwater, the diving beetle traps a bubble of air under its wing cases.

GILLS
This damselfly nymph lives underwater and uses fanlike gills at the tip of its abdomen to get some air. The gills have a large surface area and can absorb enough oxygen from the water to keep the nymph breathing until it becomes an adult.

Scents and Sense Ability

LIKE HUMANS, INSECTS use their senses—smell, touch, taste, sight, and hearing—to assemble a picture of the world around them. Much of this information is filtered through their hard-working antennae, which enable insects to smell, touch, and hear.

Sight can be a complicated thing for insects—they rely on compound eyes that may have a total of 56,000 lenses, each one recording a slightly different view! Many insects also have ocelli, a small group of eyes on the top of their heads that help with balance, flight, and light detection.

Insects taste food before they eat it, using sense organs clustered around the mouth. The most important of these are the palps. Flies and butterflies get extra help in this department from sense organs on...their feet! This way, they know when something they land on is good to eat.

Most insects rely on their antennae and the fine hairs that cover the body to help them tune in to sounds. But insects such as grasshoppers have something close to human hearing—they use earlike organs called tympana.

Insect view

Human view

NECTAR AHEAD!
Many insects have eyes that are sensitive to ultraviolet light, so they see things invisible to us. We may see a patch of flowers and nothing more. But nectar-drinkers, such as bees, butterflies, and wasps, see landing patterns that announce: "This way to a good meal!"

EARS ON THEIR BELLIES
Insects have hearing organs on their thorax, abdomen, or front legs instead of their head. The young lubber locusts (below) have tympana on their abdomen. Tympana work like human ears. A thin skin stretches between the sense receptors. When sound waves vibrate against the skin, the receptors relay the vibrations to the brain, which translates them into sound.

HANDS ON
Follow That Scent

Ants use antennae to actually sniff out food. Try this to see ants in action.

❶ Place a 12-inch (30-cm) circle of paper on flat ground near an anthill. Put a spoonful of jam outside the circle, away from the anthill, and wait for the ants to discover it. The first ants will leave a scent trail that tells the others where to find the food.

❷ While some ants are feeding, gently rotate the circle by 90°. The ants on the paper will follow the scent left by the others, but once they reach the ground, the scent and the jam won't be there. Use a magnifying glass to see how their antennae help them rediscover their lost snack.

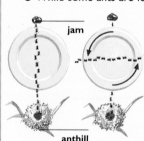

jam

anthill

DOUBLE DUTY
This weevil has thin, clubbed antennae at the end of its snout. When it bores into nuts or grain, the antennae help the insect decide if it's found food or a good place to lay eggs.

BODY HEAT
Adult fleas are sensitive to heat. They use their antennae to sense the body heat of a passing mammal or the presence of carbon dioxide, a gas breathed out by mammals. They then hop on for a meal.

TUNING IN
The most important sense organs that an insect has are the antennae on its head. These multipurpose super sensors let insects smell the world around them, as well as touch and hear it.

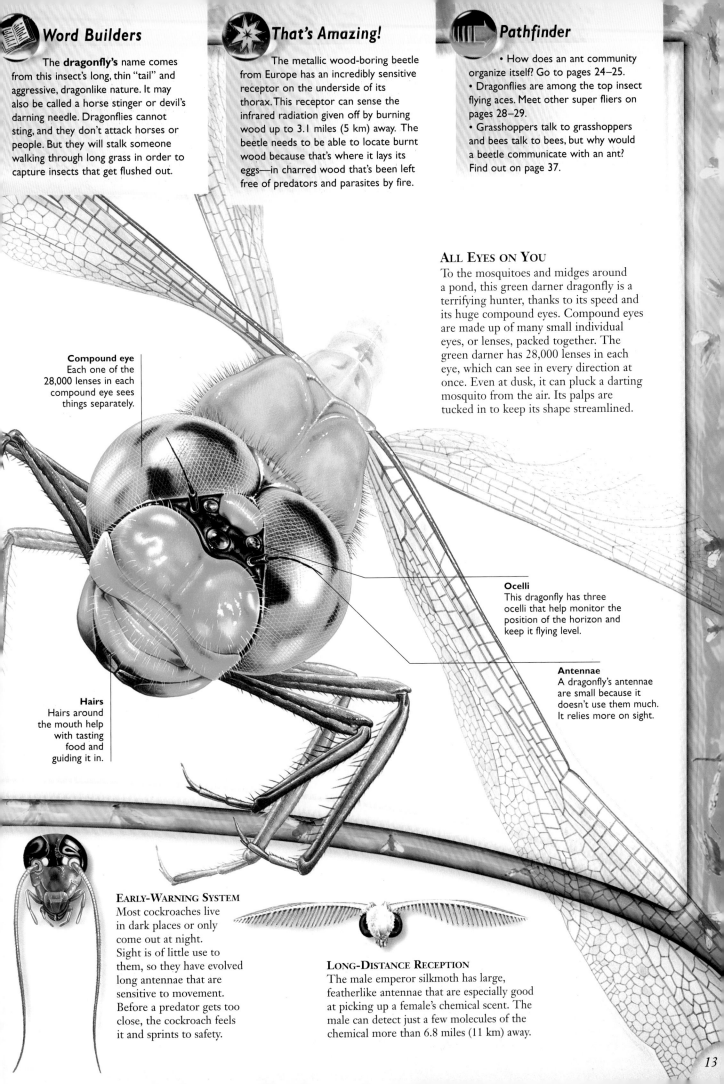

Word Builders

The **dragonfly's** name comes from this insect's long, thin "tail" and aggressive, dragonlike nature. It may also be called a horse stinger or devil's darning needle. Dragonflies cannot sting, and they don't attack horses or people. But they will stalk someone walking through long grass in order to capture insects that get flushed out.

That's Amazing!

The metallic wood-boring beetle from Europe has an incredibly sensitive receptor on the underside of its thorax. This receptor can sense the infrared radiation given off by burning wood up to 3.1 miles (5 km) away. The beetle needs to be able to locate burnt wood because that's where it lays its eggs—in charred wood that's been left free of predators and parasites by fire.

Pathfinder

• How does an ant community organize itself? Go to pages 24–25.
• Dragonflies are among the top insect flying aces. Meet other super fliers on pages 28–29.
• Grasshoppers talk to grasshoppers and bees talk to bees, but why would a beetle communicate with an ant? Find out on page 37.

ALL EYES ON YOU

To the mosquitoes and midges around a pond, this green darner dragonfly is a terrifying hunter, thanks to its speed and its huge compound eyes. Compound eyes are made up of many small individual eyes, or lenses, packed together. The green darner has 28,000 lenses in each eye, which can see in every direction at once. Even at dusk, it can pluck a darting mosquito from the air. Its palps are tucked in to keep its shape streamlined.

Compound eye
Each one of the 28,000 lenses in each compound eye sees things separately.

Ocelli
This dragonfly has three ocelli that help monitor the position of the horizon and keep it flying level.

Antennae
A dragonfly's antennae are small because it doesn't use them much. It relies more on sight.

Hairs
Hairs around the mouth help with tasting food and guiding it in.

EARLY-WARNING SYSTEM

Most cockroaches live in dark places or only come out at night. Sight is of little use to them, so they have evolved long antennae that are sensitive to movement. Before a predator gets too close, the cockroach feels it and sprints to safety.

LONG-DISTANCE RECEPTION

The male emperor silkmoth has large, featherlike antennae that are especially good at picking up a female's chemical scent. The male can detect just a few molecules of the chemical more than 6.8 miles (11 km) away.

13

Egg, Nymph, Adult

ALL INSECTS start out life as eggs. After mating, many females will try to lay their eggs close to a food source. That way, the young will have plenty to eat when they hatch from the eggs. Like all babies, insect young grow—but their exoskeletons cannot. The insect's solution is to molt, or shed, its exoskeleton. A new exoskeleton has already formed beneath the old one. With each molt, the insect changes size and shape until it becomes an adult. This is called metamorphosis, and in some species, it can take an awfully long time. The periodical cicada takes 17 years!

When some insects hatch, they already look a little like their parents. These young, called nymphs, go through a simple metamorphosis—they change, or mature, gradually until adulthood. Nymphs of some species—like silverfish, bedbugs, and aphids—may look almost exactly like their parents. Others look less like the adults. Dragonfly and damselfly nymphs are so different from their parents that they live underwater before crawling onto land for their final molt into adulthood. Nymphs of some winged insects have wing buds at the top of the thorax. These buds grow larger as the nymph grows, but they aren't ready to use until the insect hits maturity.

CARING PARENT
This shield bug is protecting her young. If a predator comes too close, she will try to scare it away. This is unusual behavior in insects. Most abandon their eggs once they have laid them. The eggs are usually tough and well hidden, so they often don't come to any harm.

A soft-shelled adult leafhopper pulls free of its old exoskeleton.

MALE AND FEMALE
The size difference between males and females is easy to see with these mantids. The male mantid (behind) is usually smaller and lighter, so he can fly around searching for a mate. The female's greater size is needed to make room for her eggs.

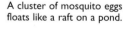

A cluster of mosquito eggs floats like a raft on a pond.

EGGS-TRAVAGANZA
Insect eggs come in many shapes, sizes, and colors. The number of eggs also varies among different insects. A female spider-hunting wasp produces between 20 and 40 eggs in her lifetime, while a termite queen can lay more than 10 million.

The females of many cockroach species make a case to protect their eggs.

Word Builders

• **Molt** comes from the Latin word *mutare*, "to change." Molting is a dangerous time for an insect because it can't really defend itself without its hard outer covering. Most hide during this period and finish within an hour. Some timber beetles, though, take several days.

• **Metamorphosis** comes from two ancient Greek words—*meta*, meaning "change," and *morphe*, meaning "form or shape."

That's Amazing!

Some nymphs wear several different disguises on the way to becoming adults. When a young Australian prickly insect hatches, it looks like a fierce bull ant. As it grows and molts, it begins to look like a piece of flaky eucalyptus bark. Eventually, when it is fully grown, it resembles a dead eucalyptus leaf.

Pathfinder

• There are two ways for an insect to get from egg to adult. Simple metamorphosis is one way. What is the other? Go to pages 16–17.

• People call all kinds of insects "bugs," but only certain types really qualify. Find out what it takes to be a true bug on pages 18–19.

• Compare an insect's life cycle with a spider's. Turn to pages 54–55.

HANDS ON

Cicada Search

If you live in a warm part of the world and you go looking for cicadas in midsummer, you will probably find them. This is when most cicada nymphs emerge from their underground homes, climb up the closest tree, molt one last time, and then start singing to attract a mate. That's the first clue to locating cicadas—their call. Next, look for the molted skins of the nymphs (right), which will be left on trees and shrubs near ground level. You will probably discover some adults nearby. After you have studied your cicada, let it go near where you found it—it won't survive for long in captivity.

The adult leafhopper, with its exoskeleton hardened.

A leafhopper nymph gets ready to shed its last exoskeleton.

GROWING PAINS

A leafhopper nymph finds a hiding place to make its final molt. By expanding and contracting its abdomen, the nymph forces air into its body to split the old exoskeleton. In a difficult move, the scarlet-and-green adult leafhopper climbs free and uses the extra air to stretch its new, soft exoskeleton. When this hardens, the air is released and there is space to grow into. Blood pumps through the veins of the leafhopper's wings to stretch them out before they harden.

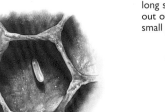

A single honeybee egg is laid in each cell of the honeycomb.

Lacewing eggs on long stalks stay out of reach of small predators.

A ladybug lays her bright yellow eggs on a leaf.

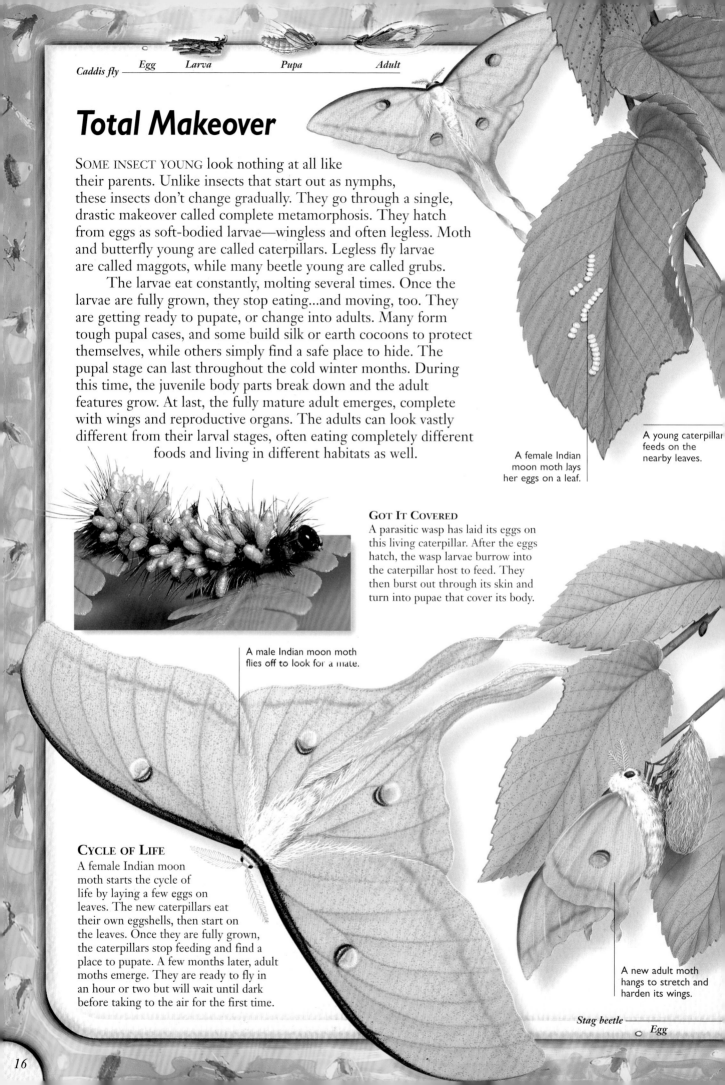

Total Makeover

SOME INSECT YOUNG look nothing at all like their parents. Unlike insects that start out as nymphs, these insects don't change gradually. They go through a single, drastic makeover called complete metamorphosis. They hatch from eggs as soft-bodied larvae—wingless and often legless. Moth and butterfly young are called caterpillars. Legless fly larvae are called maggots, while many beetle young are called grubs.

The larvae eat constantly, molting several times. Once the larvae are fully grown, they stop eating...and moving, too. They are getting ready to pupate, or change into adults. Many form tough pupal cases, and some build silk or earth cocoons to protect themselves, while others simply find a safe place to hide. The pupal stage can last throughout the cold winter months. During this time, the juvenile body parts break down and the adult features grow. At last, the fully mature adult emerges, complete with wings and reproductive organs. The adults can look vastly different from their larval stages, often eating completely different foods and living in different habitats as well.

A female Indian moon moth lays her eggs on a leaf.

A young caterpillar feeds on the nearby leaves.

GOT IT COVERED
A parasitic wasp has laid its eggs on this living caterpillar. After the eggs hatch, the wasp larvae burrow into the caterpillar host to feed. They then burst out through its skin and turn into pupae that cover its body.

A male Indian moon moth flies off to look for a mate.

CYCLE OF LIFE
A female Indian moon moth starts the cycle of life by laying a few eggs on leaves. The new caterpillars eat their own eggshells, then start on the leaves. Once they are fully grown, the caterpillars stop feeding and find a place to pupate. A few months later, adult moths emerge. They are ready to fly in an hour or two but will wait until dark before taking to the air for the first time.

A new adult moth hangs to stretch and harden its wings.

Word Builders

• **Larva** is a Latin word that means "ghost." It is the term used for the young of many insects. This is because larvae are often very pale and so look a little like ghosts.
• **Cocoon** comes from *coco*, a French word for "shell." A cocoon is a shell-like covering of silk, with mud, wood, or leaves, that protects the helpless pupa while it turns into an adult insect.

That's Amazing!

Larvae are born to eat. From the moment they hatch, they feed as much as they can. Some caterpillars grow dramatically over a short period of time. For instance, the oak silk moth caterpillar balloons from just 0.2 inches (5 mm) in length to nearly 5 inches (12.7 cm) in length. That's 12,000 times its original size—all in just three weeks.

Pathfinder

• Where does silk come from? Find out on page 23.
• Learn how a bee goes through a total makeover in the hive on pages 26–27.
• What other kinds of insect parasites are there? Go to pages 34–35.

LARVAE EATING HABITS

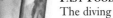

SAFE HAVEN
After spending seven years as a larva burrowing through the trunk of an oak tree, a young jewel beetle formed a small chamber in which to pupate. It has now emerged as an adult, so its new exoskeleton is soft.

This caterpillar has molted four or five times.

A caterpillar pupates inside a silk cocoon for several months.

HEALTHY SNACK
After a hawk moth larva hatches, it must eat its eggshell or it will die. The shell has chemicals that stimulate the larva to start feeding. Many insect eggshells hold nutrients and make a good first meal.

FAST FOOD
The diving beetle grub is long and thin so it can zip through water to catch prey. Its long, needle-sharp mandibles are powerful enough to spear small fish.

LEGGY LARVA
The grub of the seven-spot ladybug needs strong legs to climb after the aphids that it feeds on.

ALL YOU CAN EAT
Blowfly maggots don't need legs. They hatch directly on their food—rotting animals—and legs would get in the way. Their streamlined shape lets them burrow quickly into decaying flesh.

GET A GRIP
The large caterpillar of the hercules moth has to hang on tight when feeding on leaves high up in trees. Patches of tiny hooks at the tips of its prolegs give it a strong grip.

HANDS ON

Insect Care and Feeding

It's easy to keep an insect for closer study. Just follow these tips for making your subject feel comfortable.

❶ Use a glass jar or plastic container. Punch holes in the lid so the insect can breathe.

❷ Provide a small dish with damp tissue, so the insect won't dry out. Add twigs or leaves for climbing insects.

❸ For longer stays, identify the insect and find out what it likes to eat. What else does it need?

❹ When you're finished, release the insect where you originally found it.

 Larva   *Pupa*   *Adult*

THORNY DEVILS
The 2,300 species of treehoppers have some of the most bizarre shapes and colors of all the bugs. These thorny treehoppers have developed a spiky thorax. This helps them look like the sharp thorns on plants in the tropical rain forest where they live, so predators will avoid them.

Going Buggy

WE CALL A LOT of insects and other crawly things "bugs," but that name really refers to only one particular group of insects. The insect world is divided into separate groups called orders, and true bugs—like bedbugs and stinkbugs—belong to the order Hemiptera. Cicadas, aphids, treehoppers, and leafhoppers are in this order, too.

While many of the creatures in this order look quite different from one another, most have one feature in common: their mouthparts. Bugs don't have jaws for biting or chewing—instead they have special mouthparts for piercing and sucking up liquids. These mouthparts, shaped like hollow needles, are contained in a long, thin beak.

True bugs can be found all over the world. Most are terrestrial (land-dwelling), but there are plenty of aquatic (water-dwelling) bugs, too. Many bugs feed on plant juices, while some feed on other insects, making them useful in pest control. Still others suck the blood of animals and people, and some pass on diseases via their mouthparts as they feed.

MOTHER AND YOUNG
Many bugs live in groups, with adults and nymphs mixed in together. The colorful leafhopper bug pictured above is the adult. The white tufted creatures are nymphs. Their spiky appearance and unpleasant taste keep predators away.

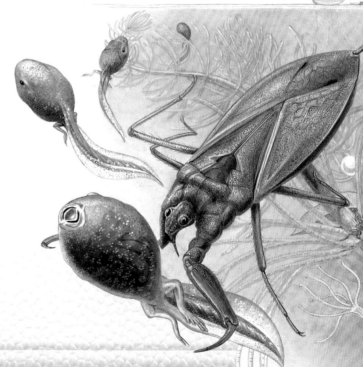

NO JOKE
A jester bug uses its needlelike mouthparts to suck nectar from a flower. When the bug is not feeding, its mouthparts stay inside the beak, tucked away in a special groove running along the underside of its body.

PUTTING INSECTS IN ORDER
Entomologists divide insects into about 30 different orders. The insects in each order have certain features in common, such as sucking mouthparts in bugs. Here are some of the best-known orders.

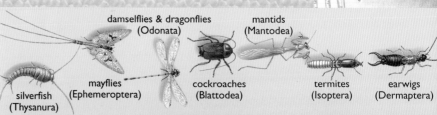

damselflies & dragonflies
(Odonata)

mantids
(Mantodea)

silverfish
(Thysanura)

mayflies
(Ephemeroptera)

cockroaches
(Blattodea)

termites
(Isoptera)

earwigs
(Dermaptera)

Word Builders

Hemiptera comes from the ancient Greek *hemi*, meaning "half," and *ptera*, meaning "wings." Many bugs in this order look "half-winged" because their wingtips are transparent. The true bugs are often split into two subgroups. The Homoptera feed on plants and hold their wings up like a roof over their back. The Heteroptera may feed on insects, animals, and humans, and their wings are held flat.

That's Amazing!

The common aphid is one of the fastest reproducing animals on Earth. When an aphid is born, it already has a baby developing inside. If it were not for insect-eaters such as ladybugs, spiders, and birds, the world would be overrun by aphids. Just one could result in 10 quintillion offspring in as little as six months. That would form a column of aphids 3 feet (1 m) wide from Earth to the Moon.

Pathfinder

• How does a white waxy treehopper nymph turn into a brightly colored treehopper adult? Go to pages 14–15.
• A ladybug is called a bug, but it isn't one. Find out what kind of insect it really is on pages 20–21.
• Discover the trick water striders use to walk on water on page 40.

WATER WORLD

Ponds can teem with bugs living both in and on top of the water's surface. Below, a water scorpion hangs suspended among the weeds, grabbing at a passing tadpole with its powerful front legs. Its long, tail-like breathing tube pierces the surface, providing a ready supply of oxygen. On the right, a water boatman paddles through the water with legs like oars. Immediately above it, two water striders stand on the pond's surface, one making a meal of a hover fly.

INSIDE STORY

Bug-ology

People who study insects are called entomologists. Because there are so many different kinds of insects living in a wide variety of habitats throughout the world, entomologists can find themselves doing lots of different things—from teaching farmers new means of pest control to collecting rainforest specimens that might provide cures for diseases like malaria and cancer. Scientists say there are still millions of animal species out there, just waiting to be identified. Since most of these species are insects, you might say that entomologists have got their work cut out for them.

grasshoppers, ckets & katydids (Orthoptera)

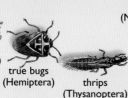
lice (Phthiraptera)

stick insects (Phasmida)

true bugs (Hemiptera)

thrips (Thysanoptera)

lacewings (Neuroptera)

beetles (Coleoptera)

fleas (Siphonaptera)

flies (Diptera)

caddis flies (Trichoptera)

moths & butterflies (Lepidoptera)

ants, bees & wasps (Hymenoptera)

Beetle Mania

IF INSECTS ARE the most successful creatures in the animal world, then beetles have to be the most successful insects. There are more than 350,000 different members of the order Coleoptera, and entomologists think there are still hundreds of thousands more to be identified.

While beetles vary greatly in shape and size, just about all of them have bodies that are heavily armored like little tanks. They have extra-thick exoskeletons as well as elytra—hardened wing cases—that protect delicate body parts like flying wings. The extra weight may slow beetles down a little, but their tough exteriors are good shields against predators.

Beetles have powerful biting and chewing mouthparts that can tackle almost any kind of food. The plant-eaters among them are often extremely picky about what kinds of leaves, flowers, pollen, or bark they will eat. Some beetles are skilled predators that hunt for small animals, including fish and other insects. Still others feed on the bodies of dead animals or on animal droppings. If they didn't, the world would be a much dirtier and smellier place.

THE SWARM
It's the end of summer, and these ladybugs (which are beetles, not bugs) have swarmed to find a sheltered hibernation spot for winter. This behavior is called aggregation. Sometimes, swarms of ladybugs can contain thousands of individuals. But they are harmless—even beneficial—unlike a swarm of locusts.

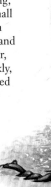
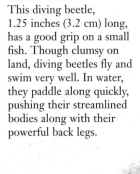

TAKE A DIVE
This diving beetle, 1.25 inches (3.2 cm) long, has a good grip on a small fish. Though clumsy on land, diving beetles fly and swim very well. In water, they paddle along quickly, pushing their streamlined bodies along with their powerful back legs.

Metallic wood borer

- The word **beetle** comes from the Old English word *bitula*, which means "biter."
- During the Middle Ages in Europe, many crops were destroyed by aphids. Just when the people thought they would starve, swarms of **ladybugs** appeared and ate the aphids. In thanks, the people named them "Our Lady bugs" after Mary, the mother of Jesus.

Some of the strongest insects in the world belong to the scarab beetle family. It has been calculated that a rhinoceros beetle can carry 350 times its own weight. In human terms, this is the same as carrying more than 34,000 pounds (15,422 kg), or three bull elephants! Rhinoceros beetles can manage this incredible feat because of their extremely thick exoskeleton and very efficient muscles.

- Wasps and weevils are also helpful insects. What do they do? Go to pages 26 and 32.
- Some beetles have a taste for dung. Find out which beetles like to eat dead bodies on page 34.

BEETLE BAZAAR

Beetles come in many colors, shapes, and sizes, depending on their lifestyle and needs.

STREAMLINED

This rove beetle is small and slender, just the right shape for squeezing between twigs and leaves as it hunts for food amidst the leaf litter where it lives.

HANDS ON

Make a Pitfall Trap

Small crawling insects can be hard to spot, especially when they are active at night, like many beetles. One way to meet the crawlers in your backyard is to build a pitfall trap to catch them.

❶ Place a layer of damp tissue paper, some leaves, and twigs in an empty can with the top removed.

❷ Dig a hole in the ground and place the can inside the hole so the open end is level with the soil.

❸ Arrange four stones around the can and lay a flat piece of wood on top of the stones. This will let insects in, but keep rain and larger animals out.

❹ Check the trap throughout the day. The insects you catch in the morning will be different from those you'll catch at night. Your catch will change with the seasons, too.

❺ Let the insects go once you've finished looking at them.

COLOR GUARD

In the creature world, bright colors often warn predators that prey tastes bad or stings. This brightly colored bee-eating beetle fools predators into staying away—even though it is harmless.

HAIR TUFTS

Some beetles have tufts of hair all over their back, like this African jewel beetle. The hairs break up the outline of the beetle's body, and may make it more difficult to spot.

ON A ROLL

These male and female dung beetles have shaped some animal droppings into a ball and are rolling it toward their burrow. The female will lay one or more eggs in it, and eventually the new larvae will hatch and eat the dung ball up. These beetles do a very important job. Australia had to import some from Africa because the local dung beetles couldn't cope with all the droppings piling up from the cattle and sheep that had been brought into the country.

LONG HORNS

The antennae of this South American longhorn beetle are 3 inches (7.5 cm) long. With these antennae, it can locate a mate or food from more than 2 miles (3.2 km) away.

Goliath beetle

Vaporer moth
caterpillar

Puss moth
caterpillar

Monarch caterpillar

Leave Me Alone!
Some caterpillars are not as defenseless as they seem. The vaporer moth caterpillar has hairs that irritate the skin and make a nasty mouthful. Packed with toxic chemicals, the bright monarch caterpillar can kill its predators. The puss moth, when disturbed, raises its head and flicks two rear whips from side to side. As a last resort, it sprays formic acid.

Monarchs on the Move
These monarch butterflies gather every fall in North America. Then millions of them migrate south to California, U.S.A., and Mexico to avoid the freezing winter. Some travel thousands of miles and cover up to 80 miles (129 km) a day.

Flights of Fancy

BUTTERFLIES ARE SOME of the insect world's most valued ambassadors to people. Nearly everyone loves their brilliant colors and delicate, fluttering wings. Actually, butterflies are just a small portion of the 150,000-plus species that make up the order Lepidoptera moths! Moths get much less publicity than their colorful cousins. They are usually small and drab, camouflaged to look like bark or leaves when they rest. Most are nocturnal (active at night) and have developed acute senses of smell and hearing. Still, there are exceptions to the rule. Some moths are diurnal (active during the day) and vibrantly colored. And some butterflies have dull, brown underwings for camouflage so they look like dead leaves when they're sitting still.

Lepidopteran young and adults have different eating habits. Both butterflies and moths start out as soft-bodied caterpillars with strong chewing jaws. The slow-moving caterpillars make easy pickings for predators, so they've evolved ways to protect themselves (see above). During a complete metamorphosis, most caterpillars' mouthparts re-form into a long, thin mouthpart called a proboscis. With the proboscis, an adult usually feeds only on liquids.

Things on Wings
Looked at under a microscope, the wing of a moth or butterfly—such as this peacock butterfly—reveals thousands of scales, all overlapping like the shingles on a roof. The scales of each species are different shapes, colors, and sizes, allowing the members of a species to identify each other.

Which Is Which?

Antennae...
If you're trying to tell a butterfly from a moth, look at the antennae first. All butterflies have thin, threadlike antennae that are clubbed at the tips, as seen on this marine blue. They also always have a proboscis, which uncurls to feed on nectar.

Proboscises, Too
Moths' antennae can be straight or feathery, like those of this ornate tiger moth. Most species also have curled proboscises. Some have short, stabbing mouthparts. Others, which have none at all, cannot eat and only live long enough to breed

Word Builders

• **Butterfly** comes from the name given to the yellow brimstone butterfly in England between 400 and 500 years ago, when it used to be known as the "butter-colored fly."

• **Migration** comes from the Latin word *migrare*, "to change." It means to travel from one area to another, usually to find a better situation. Some beetles migrate just a few inches, while certain butterflies travel 1,800 miles (2,900 km).

That's Amazing!

Not all butterflies and moths are vegetarians. Several swallowtails suck up the rotting flesh of animals. South American heliconiid butterflies like to sip on urine. And the vampire moth from Asia has a dagger-like proboscis that it uses to suck the blood of its victims, including humans.

Pathfinder

• How does a caterpillar turn into a moth? Go to pages 16–17.
• Why would one butterfly want to look like another? Learn more about it on page 43.
• Find out what humans use spider silk for on page 48.

BATHING BEAUTY

A boldly colored heliconiid mimic butterfly spreads its wings to bask in the sun while feeding on some flowers. The undersides of its wings are surprisingly drab, and in its usual resting position—with wings folded straight up over its back—predators are less likely to take notice. This South American butterfly feeds on liquid nectar, using its uncurled proboscis. It can also eat some solid pollen food.

INSIDE STORY

Wearing Caterpillar Spit

The next time your mother puts on a nice silk blouse, think of this: she's wearing caterpillar spit.

Silk is made from the material that silkworm caterpillars use to make their cocoons. When the caterpillars are ready to pupate, they make a special saliva that solidifies into thread when it hits the air. This thread is the strongest of all natural fibers—a thread of silk can be stronger than the same size thread of some kinds of steel. It takes about three days for the caterpillars to spin their cocoons. Once the cocoons are finished, silk farmers bake them in an oven, killing the insects inside. Next, they drop the cocoons in boiling water. The cocoons unravel into single strands that are then twisted together to make silk thread, ready to weave into cloth.

COLOR CONFUSION

Not all moths are drab. This colorful creature may look like a butterfly, but it is a day-flying moth from Madagascar. Like almost all moths, it rests with wings spread flat. It also has straight antennae.

RESTING POSITION

Very few moths can fold their wings the way this 88 butterfly does. Butterflies rest with wings folded up over their backs. Unlike most, the undersides of the 88's wings are brightly colored, while the upper surfaces are drab.

Soldier
big-headed ant

Worker
big-headed ant

Queen
big-headed ant

Male
big-headed ant

High Society

ANTS. YOU SEE THEM everywhere, but do you really know what goes on inside that anthill? Members of the order Hymenoptera, like bees and wasps, ants are social insects—that means they work together for the survival of the colony. The smallest ant colonies have a few dozen members, but the largest can be huge. Japanese wood ants can form groups of more than 300 million individuals in underground nests bigger than 490 football fields! Most ants build nests in wood, on plants, or out of soil—and these can be above or below ground, or even up in trees. But some species, such as driver and army ants, are nomadic and never stay in one place for long.

Nearly every ant colony has two castes, or types, of ants— the queen and the workers, who are all females. The few males in the colony exist only to mate with a new queen to start a new nest. They die soon afterward. The queen's job is to lay eggs, while the workers take care of all other business. Large workers, called majors, or soldiers, defend the nest. Medium-sized ants concentrate on building the nest or foraging for food. Some ant species gather almost anything—dead or alive—while others prefer specific seeds, fungi, or sweet plant and animal secretions. The smallest ants in the colony usually stay inside to nurse the young or clean the nest.

BIG BAD BULLDOG
One of the biggest and toughest of all ants is the Australian bulldog ant. It eats all kinds of plant foods, but it is also a ferocious hunter with huge mandibles that can deliver a painful bite to humans—and a lethal one to insects. After ambushing its katydid prey, this bulldog ant has swiftly killed and butchered it. All that's left of lunch is the katydid's head.

SOUP DU JOUR
The cups formed by the leaves of a pitcher plant are full of digestive juices. Most insects that fall in will drown and be digested by the plant. But some can survive. Here, an ant has dived in, probably to gnaw apart the cricket. Big insects take so long to digest that the plant's juices can turn bad. By removing the cricket, the ant will stop a case of plant indigestion.

GOOD NEIGHBORS

Ants can be social with a variety of different ants as well as other insects—and even plants.

ANT AND APHID
Red ants and aphids know how to keep each other happy. The ants aggressively protect the aphids from predators. The ants reward themselves by feasting on honeydew, a sweet liquid produced by the aphids.

Word Builders

A **species** is a group of living organisms that are similar and can usually breed only with one another. Scientists organize species into larger groups, called **genera**, which are made up of individual species. Genera are arranged into groups called **families**, which share certain traits, even though they can look very different from one another.

That's Amazing!

Some large honeypot worker ants spend their entire adult lives hanging from the nest's ceiling. During the rainy season in the semidesert regions where they live, the workers are stuffed full of water and nectar by the rest of the colony. Their abdomens get so swollen, they can't move. In the dry season, these living honeypots spit up this food for their nestmates to eat.

Pathfinder

• How do ants get from their nest to food and back again without losing the trail? Find out on page 12.
• Ants have their own way of saying hello. Learn what it is on page 36.
• What would you do if a column of driver ants hit town? Go to page 40.

INSIDE STORY

Atta Girls!

Leaf-cutter ants of the genus *Atta* are the Houdinis of the animal world. No other creature is more skilled at escaping from captivity than they are. Zookeepers brave enough to keep captive colonies have to build special display cases, complete with moats of running water so the ants can't swim to freedom. And the glass enclosure walls must be painted with special slippery chemicals to keep the ants from climbing out.

If one queen were to get free in a part of the U.S.A. where leaf-cutters have no natural enemies, she could produce more than 32 quadrillion (that's 32,000,000,000,000,000!) new queens in just five years. This would do untold damage to the local plants. And if each of those queens survived to establish nests with 100,000 workers each, there would be enough ants to bury the entire U.S.A. 110 feet (33.5 m) deep in insects!

FUNGUS FOOD FACTORY

Leaf-cutter ants must go to a lot of trouble to make a meal. Medium-sized workers cut off pieces of leaves and carry them back to the nest. Small workers hitch rides on the leaves to protect their nestmates from parasitic flies. They leave a pile at the front door, where soldiers with massive heads and jaws stand guard. Other workers take the leaves below. They chew them up and mix them with saliva to make a compost for growing a special fungus that will feed the colony.

ANT AND PLANT

Some plants and ants form special relationships. The bull's-horn acacia has hollow thorns where certain ants set up home. These ants act as security guards, chasing off anything that may harm the acacia— from beetles to cows. The ants even prune nearby plants to make sure their acacia gets enough sun.

ANT AND ANT

Amazon ants have specialized jaws for doing one thing—fighting other ants. They can't even feed themselves! Instead, they steal the young of other ant species. The young do all the work— including feeding and cleaning—for the entire Amazon colony!

Stings on Wings

Zzzzzzz...OUCH! Sound familiar? That may be what your first experience with a bee or wasp was like. Despite the pain they can cause, though, bees and wasps are among the most important members of the insect world. Plants depend on them to pollinate their flowers. If there were no bees to do this, we'd have few fruits or vegetables to eat. And if there were no wasps, our gardens and farms would teem with destructive insects.

Bees evolved from wasps, and they both belong to the order Hymenoptera. Scientists have identified more than 100,000 species, most of which have two pairs of wings, a narrow waist, biting mouthparts, and a pair of compound eyes. It is their highly developed way of life that sets them apart from other insects. While many hymenopterans can be called loners because they dig their own burrows or find holes in rotting trees, some social bees and wasps form incredibly complex societies in their hives and nests, making them among the most advanced of all the insects.

FOOD SOURCE
A solitary parasitic wasp like this sand wasp preys on other insects—normally not for herself but for her larvae! She'll catch an insect, such as a caterpillar, and lay eggs on it with a special organ called an ovipositor. Now the wasp's larvae will have fresh food when they hatch.

FITTING OUT THE NURSERY
This leaf-cutter bee has cut out a perfect semicircle of leaf, rolled it between her jaws, and now flies it back to her burrow. She uses the leaf as wallpaper to build a cell, then fills it with nectar and pollen, and lays an egg on it.

Larva
A bee larva is fed honey and pollen for five to six days, and molts five times.

Cell
Worker bees produce wax to make or repair cells, which are used to store honey and pollen or to rear young.

Pupa
Its cell capped, a larva spins a cocoon and pupates for several weeks.

Cell capping
A worker bee caps the cell of a mature larva with a wax seal.

INSIDE STORY
Insects on Pest Patrol

Insects reproduce so quickly and in such large numbers that they can easily become pests. One of the best ways to combat pests is to use their natural enemies—including other insects—to keep their numbers in check. The Chinese started using insects for pest control 2,500 years ago, but it has only become common practice worldwide within the last 30 years. After

certain insecticides were proven to harm the environment, scientists started looking for safer ways to control pests. Many parasitic wasp species are now bred and sold to farmers to kill insects, such as aphids and scale bugs, that damage crops. Ichneumon wasps like this one (left) are used to kill the larvae of wood-boring wasps, which destroy valuable timber.

Cow killer wasp

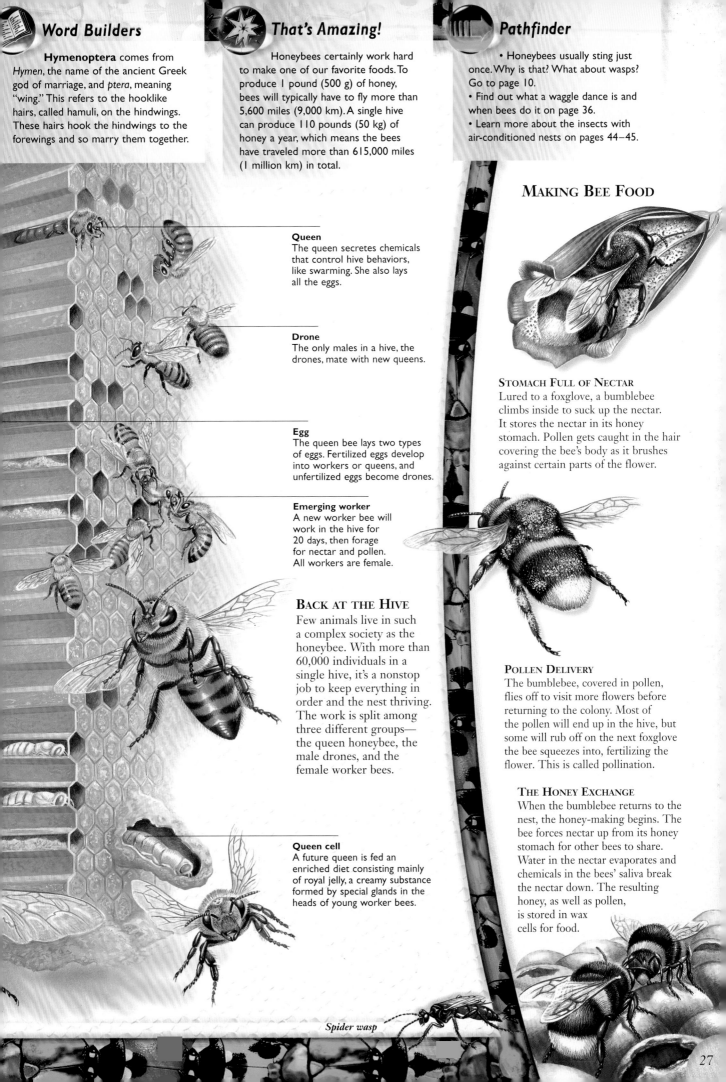

Word Builders

Hymenoptera comes from *Hymen*, the name of the ancient Greek god of marriage, and *ptera*, meaning "wing." This refers to the hooklike hairs, called *hamuli*, on the hindwings. These hairs hook the hindwings to the forewings and so marry them together.

That's Amazing!

Honeybees certainly work hard to make one of our favorite foods. To produce 1 pound (500 g) of honey, bees will typically have to fly more than 5,600 miles (9,000 km). A single hive can produce 110 pounds (50 kg) of honey a year, which means the bees have traveled more than 615,000 miles (1 million km) in total.

Pathfinder

• Honeybees usually sting just once. Why is that? What about wasps? Go to page 10.
• Find out what a waggle dance is and when bees do it on page 36.
• Learn more about the insects with air-conditioned nests on pages 44–45.

Queen
The queen secretes chemicals that control hive behaviors, like swarming. She also lays all the eggs.

Drone
The only males in a hive, the drones, mate with new queens.

Egg
The queen bee lays two types of eggs. Fertilized eggs develop into workers or queens, and unfertilized eggs become drones.

Emerging worker
A new worker bee will work in the hive for 20 days, then forage for nectar and pollen. All workers are female.

BACK AT THE HIVE

Few animals live in such a complex society as the honeybee. With more than 60,000 individuals in a single hive, it's a nonstop job to keep everything in order and the nest thriving. The work is split among three different groups— the queen honeybee, the male drones, and the female worker bees.

Queen cell
A future queen is fed an enriched diet consisting mainly of royal jelly, a creamy substance formed by special glands in the heads of young worker bees.

Spider wasp

MAKING BEE FOOD

STOMACH FULL OF NECTAR
Lured to a foxglove, a bumblebee climbs inside to suck up the nectar. It stores the nectar in its honey stomach. Pollen gets caught in the hair covering the bee's body as it brushes against certain parts of the flower.

POLLEN DELIVERY
The bumblebee, covered in pollen, flies off to visit more flowers before returning to the colony. Most of the pollen will end up in the hive, but some will rub off on the next foxglove the bee squeezes into, fertilizing the flower. This is called pollination.

THE HONEY EXCHANGE
When the bumblebee returns to the nest, the honey-making begins. The bee forces nectar up from its honey stomach for other bees to share. Water in the nectar evaporates and chemicals in the bees' saliva break the nectar down. The resulting honey, as well as pollen, is stored in wax cells for food.

The Flies Have It

THEY FEAST ON decaying flesh, pierce skin to suck blood, and can spread disease wherever they land. Whatever they're up to—even if they're just pollinating flowers—flies have an enormous impact on our world. About 100,000 different species in the order Diptera have been identified, although we notice only a few of the peskier ones.

Flies usually come in the same basic shape and size. Most are no bigger than a thumbnail, although one, called the Trinidad horse fly, can be as big as a walnut. Not all flies actually fly, but those that do have two wings. What was once the other pair has evolved into little knobs called halteres. These peg-shaped body parts are not used for propulsion but, instead, help flies keep their balance during flight. Some parasitic species don't have any wings at all, so they rely on their hosts to move them around. Because flies can't eat solid food, they have developed mouthparts that act like straws or sponges, sucking up food in a liquid form. Most have excellent eyesight and can spot the smallest movement—which is why they are so hard to swat!

Maggots are the blind and legless larvae of flies. Some eat rotting plants and animals. Some live in ponds and streams, feeding on microscopic organisms in the water. Other maggots like to lunch on the living, and that can include caterpillars, spiders, even humans.

AVIATOR'S INSTRUMENTS

Flies are expert aviators thanks to their stabilizing halteres. These peglike pieces with knobs on the end, seen here on this crane fly, used to be their back wings. The halteres vibrate very fast during flight to keep the fly's body balanced and level. Modern ships use a similar technique to keep them from rolling around too much in storms.

MIDAIR ATTACK

This giant robber fly can accelerate from 0 to 25 miles per hour (40 km/h) in just two seconds to snatch a bee out of midair. Its sharp mouthparts stab into the back of the bee's thorax, killing it instantly. But the robber fly will return to its perch before slurping up its prey—it's difficult to fly and eat at the same time.

INSIDE STORY

Mosquito Menace

Mosquitoes don't actually bite. They pierce the skin and then suck up the blood. Only female mosquitoes are bloodsuckers. The males live on nectar, but females also need blood from animals so their eggs will mature. The itchiness you feel from a bite is an allergic reaction to the chemicals the mosquito injects to make your blood flow better. It's the bite (in particular, the small organisms that live in mosquitoes) that makes these insects some of the most dangerous creatures on Earth—especially if the organism is the parasite that causes malaria. More people have died from malaria than from any other cause, including war. Each year, it kills more than two million people. Billions of dollars have been spent controlling mosquito populations, but the insect is still a menace.

Green bottle fly

Word Builders

- **Diptera** comes from the Greek words *di*, meaning "two," and *ptera*, meaning "wings." While some flies have no wings, most have two.
- **Robber flies** are super speedsters that can even catch fast dragonflies in midair. They get their name from the way they sneak up behind their victims before striking, just like a robber.

That's Amazing!

Many maggots are disease spreaders, but not all. Doctors in the 1800s learned that some feed only on rotting flesh, leaving healthy tissue behind. The doctors put the maggots on soldiers' infected wounds to eat up the rotting areas and make the wounds clean. These types of maggots are still used on certain wounds today.

Pathfinder

- How do fly larvae survive if they can't see and they can't walk? Go to page 17.
- Learn how insects keep the world clean on pages 20–21 and 34–35.
- How do flies fly? To find out, fly on over to pages 38–39.

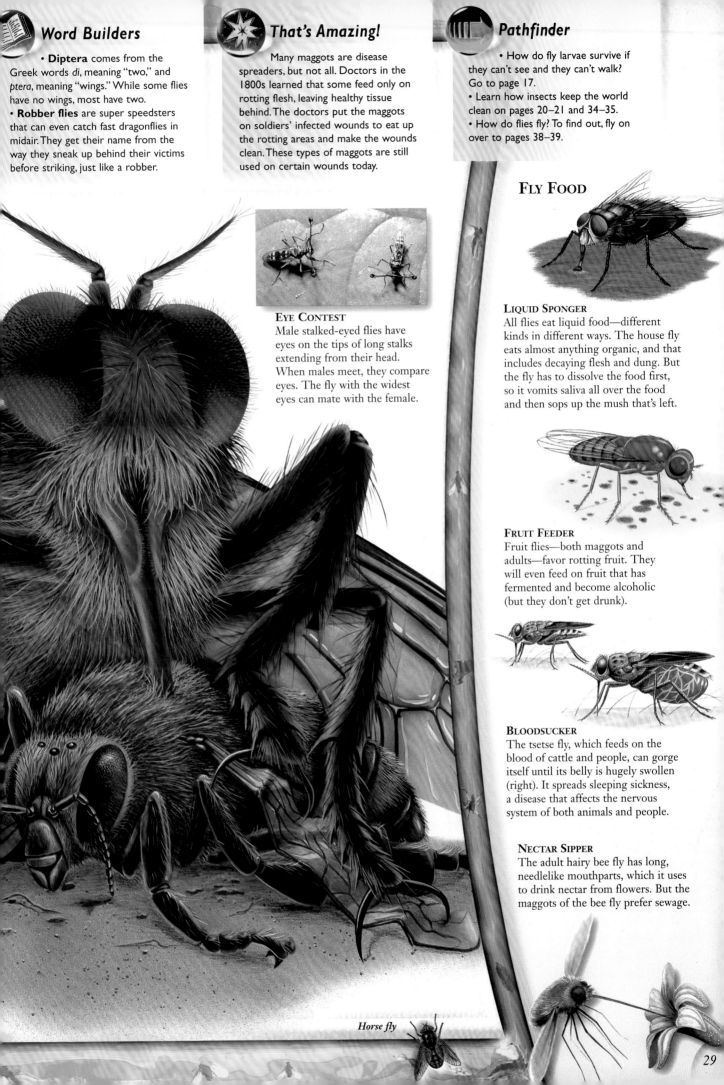

FLY FOOD

EYE CONTEST
Male stalked-eyed flies have eyes on the tips of long stalks extending from their head. When males meet, they compare eyes. The fly with the widest eyes can mate with the female.

LIQUID SPONGER
All flies eat liquid food—different kinds in different ways. The house fly eats almost anything organic, and that includes decaying flesh and dung. But the fly has to dissolve the food first, so it vomits saliva all over the food and then sops up the mush that's left.

FRUIT FEEDER
Fruit flies—both maggots and adults—favor rotting fruit. They will even feed on fruit that has fermented and become alcoholic (but they don't get drunk).

BLOODSUCKER
The tsetse fly, which feeds on the blood of cattle and people, can gorge itself until its belly is hugely swollen (right). It spreads sleeping sickness, a disease that affects the nervous system of both animals and people.

NECTAR SIPPER
The adult hairy bee fly has long, needlelike mouthparts, which it uses to drink nectar from flowers. But the maggots of the bee fly prefer sewage.

Horse fly

The World's Abuzz

NOW THAT YOU'VE met the cast of characters, watch them in action. Insects lead busy lives just as we do—but on a different scale, because they're smaller. Since there are millions upon millions of insects, though, the things they do have a huge impact on our planet and our lives. Just how do the world's insects find mates, feed themselves, and stay safe? Read on.

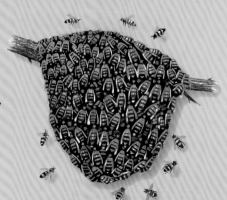

Insect-Plant Connection

PLANTS CAN BE both a home and a meal for insects. In fact, more than half of the world's insects are herbivores, or plant-eaters. But the insect-plant connection is far more complex than this. Insects pollinate flowering plants and help to recycle dead ones, turning them into rich nutrients for new plants. If not for this special give-and-take relationship, we wouldn't have biodiversity—the huge variety of plants and animals now in existence. The process whereby plants and animals help each other to evolve is known as coevolution.

In the wild, populations of plant-eating insects are kept in check by how much food they can find—and by how easily they become food for others. But humans can change this balance, especially when we plant crops. Suddenly, insects such as locusts have unlimited food without any predators to stop them. That's when insects become pests.

Not all plants sit still for the insect onslaught, however. Some species have evolved sharp spines or potent poisons to ward off plant-eaters. Other plants, like the Venus flytrap, have learned to eat the insects that try to eat them.

TRAPPED!
A fly is caught in the clutches of a Venus flytrap from Mexico. The flytrap's bright colors lure the fly, and its spine-rimmed leaves snap shut as soon as the sensitive trigger hairs are touched twice. Over the next few days, the flytrap will digest the fly, absorbing nutrients that it cannot get from the poor soil it grows in.

SPECIAL RELATIONSHIP
Without each other, the yucca moth and the yucca plant might well die out. The yucca plant counts on the moth to pollinate its flowers as the moth lays her eggs on the plant. The plant's seeds provide food for the caterpillars that hatch from the eggs, but they don't eat all the seeds. This way, the surviving seeds grow into the next generation of plants. The next generation of moths grows up too, starting the process all over again.

INSIDE STORY

Weevils to the Rescue

A water fern from Brazil was introduced into Africa, Asia, and Australia, where it had no natural enemies to keep it under control. It grew so fast that it soon choked lakes, reservoirs, and slow rivers like this one in Papua New Guinea (top). Fishermen couldn't use their boats, and mosquitoes started to breed. People tried everything to clear the fern but failed. Eventually, scientists learned about a small Brazilian weevil called *Cyrtobagous*. Its only food was the fern. After being released in the infested areas, the weevils made short work of the weeds. The river in Papua New Guinea was cleared in just three months (bottom).

Before

After

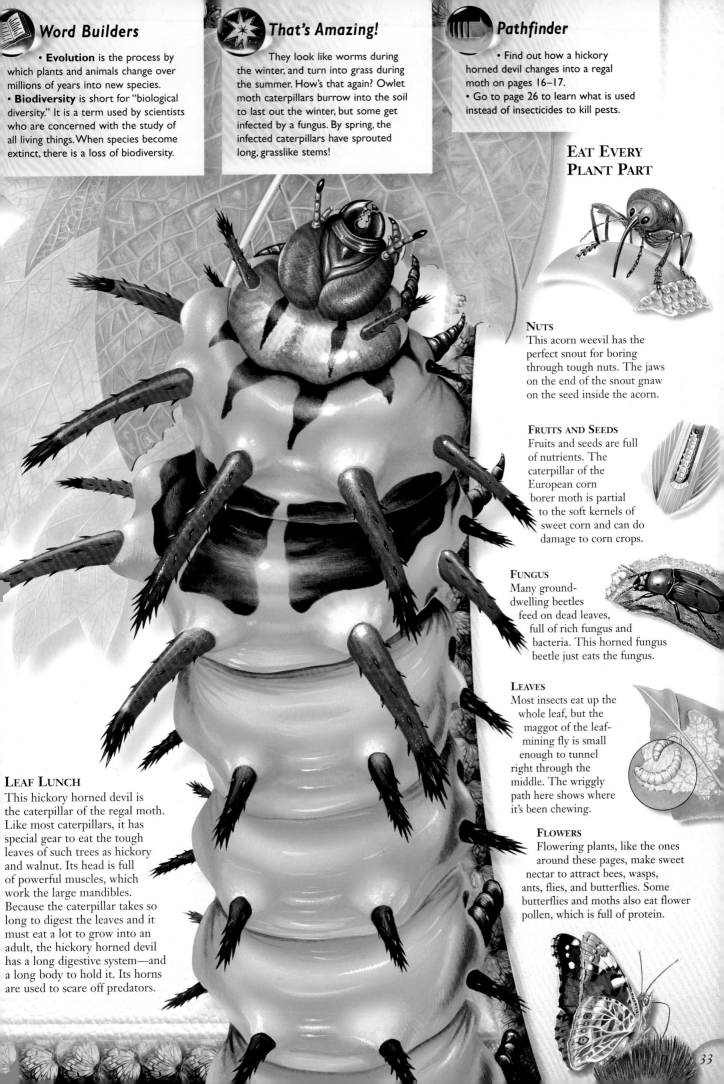

Word Builders

• **Evolution** is the process by which plants and animals change over millions of years into new species.
• **Biodiversity** is short for "biological diversity." It is a term used by scientists who are concerned with the study of all living things. When species become extinct, there is a loss of biodiversity.

That's Amazing!

They look like worms during the winter, and turn into grass during the summer. How's that again? Owlet moth caterpillars burrow into the soil to last out the winter, but some get infected by a fungus. By spring, the infected caterpillars have sprouted long, grasslike stems!

Pathfinder

• Find out how a hickory horned devil changes into a regal moth on pages 16–17.
• Go to page 26 to learn what is used instead of insecticides to kill pests.

EAT EVERY PLANT PART

NUTS
This acorn weevil has the perfect snout for boring through tough nuts. The jaws on the end of the snout gnaw on the seed inside the acorn.

FRUITS AND SEEDS
Fruits and seeds are full of nutrients. The caterpillar of the European corn borer moth is partial to the soft kernels of sweet corn and can do damage to corn crops.

FUNGUS
Many ground-dwelling beetles feed on dead leaves, full of rich fungus and bacteria. This horned fungus beetle just eats the fungus.

LEAVES
Most insects eat up the whole leaf, but the maggot of the leaf-mining fly is small enough to tunnel right through the middle. The wriggly path here shows where it's been chewing.

FLOWERS
Flowering plants, like the ones around these pages, make sweet nectar to attract bees, wasps, ants, flies, and butterflies. Some butterflies and moths also eat flower pollen, which is full of protein.

LEAF LUNCH
This hickory horned devil is the caterpillar of the regal moth. Like most caterpillars, it has special gear to eat the tough leaves of such trees as hickory and walnut. Its head is full of powerful muscles, which work the large mandibles. Because the caterpillar takes so long to digest the leaves and it must eat a lot to grow into an adult, the hickory horned devil has a long digestive system—and a long body to hold it. Its horns are used to scare off predators.

Predators, Etc.

THE WORLD PROVIDES plenty of food for insects who prefer protein—in the form of other insects and small animals such as spiders, snails, and tadpoles—to veggies. Some predators aggressively pursue their prey. Tiger beetles are the fastest hunters on six legs. The less active ground beetles hunt down slower prey like worms and caterpillars. Dragonflies are superswift hunters of the airways, swooping down and occasionally even snacking on prey in midflight.

Other predators wait for home delivery. They can simply blend in with their surroundings and grab prey that wanders within range. Or, like antlion larvae, they can be trappers. This insect lies buried beneath a funnel-shaped sand pit, waiting for an ant to stumble and fall into its huge jaws. Still other species actually attract prey with appealing odors or light sources.

Then there are scavengers, which don't hunt but, instead, live off animal wastes and carrion. Many feed on animal droppings, urine, and shed skin. Maggots and burying beetles feed on corpses, making them some of nature's most efficient recyclers. Still others, like fleas, lice, and some flies, are parasites that feed on the blood and bodily tissues of living victims.

INSECT CLEANERS
The carrion-eating sexton beetle has chewed off some rabbit meat. The female beetle will roll the piece into a ball and drag it into its burrow, ready when its larvae hatch and need a good food supply. Insects such as this beetle—that eat dead bodies or collect them for their young to eat—keep the world from piling up with rotting remains.

CARNIVORE MOUTHPARTS
Mouthparts say a lot about how these meat-eating insects feed. Tiger beetles are hunters with large jaws and teeth to catch, hold, and cut up prey. The house fly survives on liquid foods and uses a spongelike pad on its proboscis to mop them up. Assassin bugs live on liquids, too, but they suck them up with tubelike mouthparts that are tough and sharp—and must pierce prey before sucking them dry.

Tiger beetle

House fly

Assassin bug

Word Builders

• A **parasite**, from the ancient Greek *parasitos*, meaning "one who eats at the table of another," is a plant or animal that lives and feeds off another plant or animal. A parasite doesn't kill its victim but can make it very ill.
• A **parasitoid** slowly eats and kills its host. Larvae of some wasps and flies do this—they are not true parasites.

That's Amazing!

• A predatory katydid from Australia makes sure that its tree frog dinner never gets away. It pins one of the frog's hind legs down, eats the leg first, then starts on the body.
• The flambeau butterfly sips the tears of alligators, while some Asian moths drink the tears of buffaloes and people.

Pathfinder

• Learn how insects find the food they like to eat on pages 12–13.
• What scavenger keeps the world from drowning in dung and droppings? Go to pages 20–21.
• How can other insects defend themselves against predatory insects? Find out on pages 42–43.

DEADLY DECEIVER

An orchid mantis slowly changes color from white to pink and blends in almost perfectly with the flower on which it is living. Petal-shaped parts on its legs help complete the deception. It sits very still, eyeing a katydid that has been attracted to the flower. When the katydid wanders within range, the mantis will lash out, its front legs snapping shut to clamp down on the katydid with sharp spines.

INSIDE STORY

Roaches Rule!

The cockroach has been a successful scavenger for millions of years. It prefers nice warm places with plenty of food, but it can live for weeks at 39°F (4°C) and go without food for months. It will eat any food scraps, and it's also been known to snack on cardboard, the plastic insulation around electrical wire, and even its own offspring. The cockroach rests most of the time but can be very active—swimming underwater for 40 minutes or running up to 3 miles (5 km) in an hour. It can also survive radiation levels that would kill humans.

GRUB FOR A GRUB

This spider-hunting wasp avoids a tarantula's fangs by stabbing it with a long stinger that injects a paralyzing poison. The wasp will drag the victim into its burrow and lay a single egg on it. The grub that hatches will slowly devour the spider. This spider-hunting wasp is called a parasitoid because the hungry grub always kills the spider. True parasites do not actually kill their victim.

Grasshopper

Honeybee

HERBIVORE MOUTHPARTS

Plant-eaters chew or suck up their food, but their mouthparts are different from those of carnivorous insects because of the food they eat. Grasshoppers chew solid plant food. Their jaws are strong, with a sharp edge—perfect for cutting up tough grasses. Honeybees have a long proboscis for taking up nectar, and jaws that shape wax to build cells in the hive.

Contact!

PICTURE THIS: you're very little, but the world around you is huge. How do you find others of your species to let them know you're available to make more of the same? Communication makes it all happen. And insects employ a variety of means to communicate.

Many use sound and vibration. The chirps of male crickets are a familiar sound. Cicadas create an earsplitting buzz—a sign that courting season has arrived. Less obvious are the butterflies that click to each other and the lacewings and treehoppers that stamp messages on the branches they stand on. Backswimmers and water striders feel vibrations through the water with their feet.

Flying beetles, moths, and butterflies release chemicals called pheromones into the air to catch the attention of a possible mate. The male orchid bee from South America can't produce its own scent, so it uses the scent from an orchid—and females, who have special receptors on their antennae, find it irresistible.

Insects also use visual signals to attract a mate. Many butterflies and dragonflies recognize one another's markings—the males are often more colorful than the females. Picture-wing flies use their patterned wings to signal to a mate, while fireflies and glowworms use spectacular light shows for their courtship rituals.

EAU DE MOTH
This female fire-dweller micromoth has special glands on her abdomen, which help spread a male-attracting pheromone through the air. Nearby male micromoths have receptors sensitive enough to pick up just a few molecules of the scent. Most pheromones are too weak to be perceived by human noses, but a few stronger ones smell of vanilla, chocolate, musk, pineapple, or burnt wood.

GLOW IN THE DARK
With a mix of special chemicals, this female glowworm, a type of beetle, can "turn on" a light in her abdomen. This is called bioluminescence. She flashes the light on and off in a special pattern, sending a message to a male glowworm, who flashes back as he flies overhead. When lots of these insects get together, they light up whole trees and meadows.

INSIDE STORY

Singing Pets

You've heard of pet dogs, cats, and even pet snakes. But what about keeping a pet insect? In China, they've been keeping crickets as pets for more than 1,000 years. They do it mainly so they can enjoy the melodic chirping that different crickets produce, and the cages that the crickets live in can be very ornate.

Over the last few hundred years, the Chinese have also raised pet crickets for cricket fighting contests. Two males are placed in a small arena. Because they are very territorial insects, the crickets start to fight and bite at each other. They have powerful jaws, but one will usually run away before there are any serious injuries.

MORE REASONS TO TALK

ANTENNAE CHECK
Every ant nest has its own particular smell, a pheromone produced by the queen ant. When these two red ants meet, they gently touch their antennae together to check smells and see if they are from the same nest. Invading ants are quickly caught and kicked out.

DANCING IN THE DARK
Honeybees tell nestmates where food is with a special dance. In the darkness of the nest, the others must feel the movements to understand. A fast abdomen waggle means lots of nectar. The direction of the dance tells them where to look.

Word Builders

- A **territorial** insect patrols and protects a particular piece of land, or territory, from intruders.
- **Bioluminescence** (formed from the Latin *bio*, "life," and *lumen*, "light") is the ability of certain living organisms to produce light by mixing together chemicals in the body.

That's Amazing!

Deathwatch beetles lay their eggs in old timber so that larvae can end up in wood houses. When an adult beetle emerges, it taps its head on the wood. Another beetle gets the message, and the two home in on each other. In early times, this noise could be heard late at night by people who sat with dying relatives. That's how the insect was given the name "deathwatch" beetle.

Pathfinder

- Find out how insects actually pick up signals and messages from each other on pages 12–13.
- What do bees do after they've done the waggle dance and found the nectar? Go to page 27.
- How does a termite colony work? Learn all about it on pages 44–45.

GRASSHOPPER CALLING

A painted grasshopper rapidly rubs small pegs on its back legs against the hard ridges along its wings. This makes the wings vibrate, and that's what makes the loud, rasping noise that male grasshoppers are famous for. Each species has its own call. It's their way of attracting females, who pick up the call with the "ears" on their abdomens.

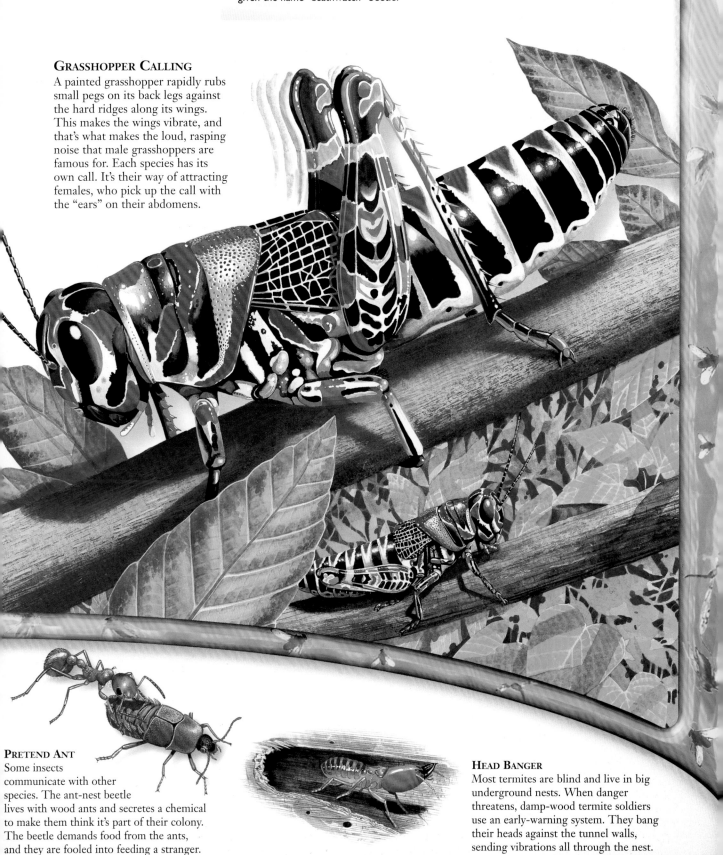

PRETEND ANT

Some insects communicate with other species. The ant-nest beetle lives with wood ants and secretes a chemical to make them think it's part of their colony. The beetle demands food from the ants, and they are fooled into feeding a stranger.

HEAD BANGER

Most termites are blind and live in big underground nests. When danger threatens, damp-wood termite soldiers use an early-warning system. They bang their heads against the tunnel walls, sending vibrations all through the nest.

Takeoff

INSECTS HAVE BEEN FLYING for more than 300 million years, since wings evolved from gills on aquatic nymphs. The first fliers probably did little more than glide, but as wing design improved, so did flying skills. Some ancient species had three pairs of wings, but most insects today have one or two pairs. Butterflies, dragonflies, bees, and wasps use both pairs as flying wings. Other insects use one pair to fly. In beetles, the other pair has evolved into tough wing cases and in flies, flight-stabilizing halteres.

Some insects are excellent aviators. Hover flies can zoom around or slow down, change direction suddenly, hover in the same spot, and even fly backward! Butterflies beat their large wings slowly, but some can fly continuously for over 100 miles (160 km). Honeybees can fly for only about 15 minutes before they need to refuel.

An insect's wings are powered by strong muscles in the thorax. Each wing connects to the thorax by a tiny plate called a sclerite. With this joint, the wing can move up or down, backward or forward, helping the insect to maneuver. A house fly beats its wings about 200 times per second; some midges make about 1,000 beats in that time.

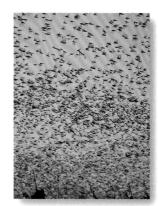

FLIGHT FOR FOOD
Having stripped an area bare of plants so there is nothing left to eat, this swarm of adult locusts takes to the air to look for more. Insects often use flight to cover large distances when searching for food. But locusts are not strong fliers. They can be blown off course by the wind, and many can drown at sea.

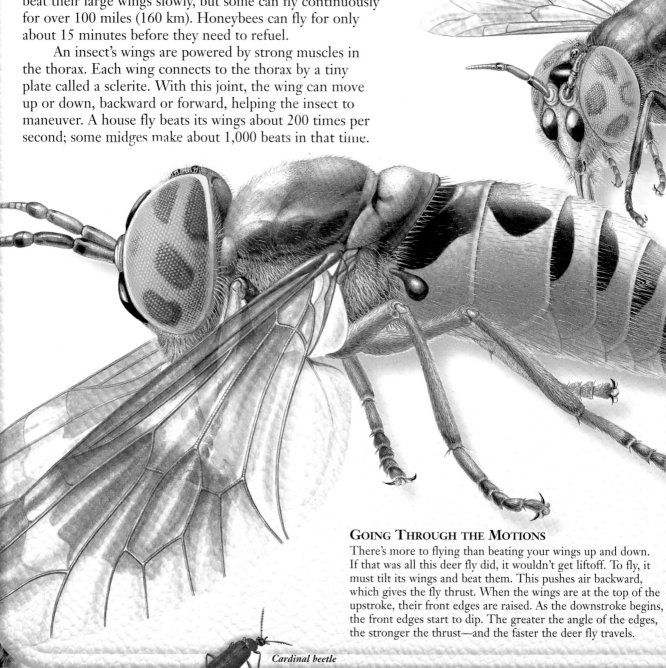

GOING THROUGH THE MOTIONS
There's more to flying than beating your wings up and down. If that was all this deer fly did, it wouldn't get liftoff. To fly, it must tilt its wings and beat them. This pushes air backward, which gives the fly thrust. When the wings are at the top of the upstroke, their front edges are raised. As the downstroke begins, the front edges start to dip. The greater the angle of the edges, the stronger the thrust—and the faster the deer fly travels.

Cardinal beetle

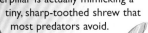
Hawk moths are fast fliers, like the birds of prey they are named after—hawks. The **elephant hawk moth** is named for its caterpillar's long, gray body and false eye spots, which make it look a little like an elephant's head. But the caterpillar is actually mimicking a tiny, sharp-toothed shrew that most predators avoid.

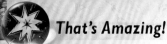
When the nymphs of some grasshoppers become too crowded, they start to change color, shape, and behavior, turning into locusts instead of grasshoppers. Once they are adults, they take to the air in huge swarms of as many as 100 billion individuals. This blizzard of insects can cover more than 2,000 miles (3,225 km).

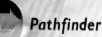
• Do you see plenty of butterflies fluttering around, but not as many moths? Learn more about it on pages 22–23.
• Why do bees swarm? Find out on page 45.

DIFFERENT WINGS

There are many types of insect wings, but most have a similar structure. Two thin sheets of chitin are sandwiched together. A network of veins running between the sheets gives them support.

UNITED THEY BEAT

Hornets have two pairs of transparent wings. The front and back wings are held together by a series of tiny hooks, so the wings beat in perfect unison.

DOUBLE OR NOTHING

The awkward size and shape of a dragonfly's wings should make it a poor flier. But the back pair beat at a slightly different speed from the front pair, increasing the dragonfly's stability during flight.

AIR PLAY

Few creatures can match the fly's aerial skill. Incredibly agile, flies can even flip themselves over while in midair, ready to land upside down on the ceiling.

GOT IT COVERED

A beetle's tough forewings act mainly as covers for its hindwings. In flight, they also work like the fixed wings of an airplane, keeping the beetle stable and giving it extra lift.

GLIDER

This grasshopper relies on a powerful leap to become airborne. Then large, fanlike hindwings unfold, helping it to glide long distances.

HOVERING HAWK MOTH

This elephant hawk moth is so heavy that it cannot land on some flowers to collect nectar. It has to keep flying in the same spot as it sips from the flower. This is hovering, an action that produces so much heat that the moth would actually cook if it didn't release the heat through its abdomen.

HANDS ON

To Catch a Flier

The best way to catch insects that fly is with a sweep net—a strong, light net with a long handle. Many insects can fly faster than you can run, so you'll improve your chances if you can trap them before they take off. Once they're in flight, the best method is to wave the net from side to side as you walk along through long grass. The second an insect flies into the net, twist your wrist so that the net's mouth points down toward the ground. The insect cannot escape then. After you have studied it, let the insect go quickly—otherwise it will use up energy flapping around, trapped in the net, and will soon become exhausted.

Cardinal beetle takeoff and flight

Pine processionary caterpillars

On the Move

NONFLYING INSECTS USE a more pedestrian method of getting around—their legs. Insects have six multijointed legs that make them very stable. They can start fast and stop suddenly without falling over. They are also very light, making it easy for them to maneuver.

Some species have special equipment, like claws or sticky pads on their feet, that allows them to climb walls or windows—or even hang from ceilings. Others have developed appendages made just for jumping. Grasshoppers have such powerful back legs that they can make leaps many times higher than their bodies. Some jumpers don't use legs at all—tiny springtails flick a special "tail," while click beetles use a peglike spring to propel themselves.

Oarlike legs make swimming easy for many aquatic insects. Dragonfly nymphs, for instance, can either paddle around or use jet propulsion. They force water out the tip of their abdomen to push themselves along.

Many kinds of larvae get along fine with no legs at all. Some, like fly larvae, simply wiggle. Others, like ant and bee larvae, have no need for legs because their food is delivered. Still others depend on limo service provided by different insects, such as bees and roaches.

DO THE ZIGZAG
When an insect walks, it moves three legs at a time. The first and third legs on one side and the middle leg on the other side all step forward together. Then it's the turn of the other three legs to step out. The end result is a slightly zigzagging walk.

INSIDE STORY

The Ants Go Marching

When 22 million African driver ants march into town, people know it's time to clear out for a while. Even though they are blind—and each one is only about 0.4 inches (1 cm) long—the insects arrive in a broad, sweeping band, and their vast numbers spell trouble for any small animal that cannot get out of the way. The minute a scout driver ant finds a grasshopper or toad, for example, it releases a chemical, and within seconds, several thousand sharp-jawed workers have completely smothered the doomed victim, pulling it apart into small pieces and carting it back to the main column of ants. In this way, they devour pests like cockroaches, scorpions, and spiders, and send snakes slithering out of their hiding places. Despite the inconvenience of leaving home, villagers in Africa tend not to mind these visits. It's a small price to pay for such a good cleaning service.

WALKING ON WATER
This water strider uses surface tension to skate on the water's surface. Hairs on its feet repel water, and this keeps the strider from piercing the water's surface. Should these hairs absorb water, the insect could no longer stay afloat.

PROTECTING
This koringkriek cricket leg isn't used for jumping away from danger. Its thick armor and spines give the cricket good defense against everything except large predatory birds and lizards.

LEGS GALORE
Insect legs come in so many shapes because they have so many functions. Each species has evolved legs to suit its lifestyle and needs—for walking, swimming, jumping, or catching food.

HUNTING
The spined front legs of a praying mantis shoot out to grab a victim in one-twentieth of a second—too fast for most to see it coming.

Word Builders

- **Surface tension** is the skin on the surface of water, which can support the light weight of leaves, twigs, and even some insects.
- **Appendage**, from the Latin *appendere*, meaning "to hang," is used to describe any body part attached to, or hanging from, one of the main body segments. An insect's antennae, legs, and wings are all appendages.

That's Amazing!

Being legless doesn't mean helpless. Take the legless larva of the stylops. It waits inside a flower's nectar store. A bee drinks the nectar—and the stylops, too. Back at the hive, the bee spits up the nectar for the next batch of bee grubs. The stylops comes too, and tucks into one of the grubs for a meal.

Pathfinder

- Members of this insect order can walk, run, jump, swim, and fly. Read all about them on pages 20–21.
- Mantises have another advantage when they go hunting—they can become invisible. Can you see how on pages 34–35?

IN A SPIN

When this flea beetle makes a jump, it shoots through the air at speeds greater than 9 miles per hour (14 km/h), spinning head-over-claws 70 times in a single second. It does all this and still manages to land feet first. The enlarged back legs hold a special jumping organ—a sliver of chitin with many muscles—that lets the beetle leap at such speeds and always land where it wants.

SWIMMING

Fringed with hairs and powered by strong muscles in the thorax, the two long legs of the diving beetle work like paddles to propel it swiftly through water.

STICKING

Fly legs are simple, but fly feet are special. Each foot has hair pads that secrete oily fluids so the fly can stick to glass and ceilings.

GRASPING

A caterpillar has jointed legs at the front and prolegs, or false legs, at the back. The prolegs have tiny hooks on their tips to help the caterpillar hold on to leaves and twigs.

Staying Alive

INSECTS—THEY'RE ON the lunch menu for many animals worldwide. It's no surprise, really, considering their sheer numbers, availability, and high protein content. But insects have evolved an array of special tricks to avoid becoming lunch. The best method is not to get noticed in the first place. Many insects stay hidden under ground. Others use camouflage to blend in with the leaves, bark, or flowers on which they're resting, or they look like leaves or twigs themselves. Some insects, like moths, may go out only under cover of darkness.

For those insects that don't stay hidden during the day, a painful sting or a toxic poison will ward off many predators. Brilliant warning colors like red, yellow, and orange tell possible attackers that this insect would be an unpleasant mouthful. Some sneaky insects pretend to be dangerous by looking like a species that really is. For example, hover flies are harmless, but they mimic, or look like, stinging yellow jackets. Certain beetles use chemical warfare. They might spray toxic chemicals at an attacker, leak irritating fluids, or even create explosive poisons.

Many insects have simply made themselves too difficult to eat. Caterpillars covered in spines or itchy hairs can't be swallowed comfortably—some have hairs that can actually choke a predator to death. The exoskeletons of several beetles are so tough that predators can't bite into them. These are the tools needed to stay alive in the creature world.

SURPRISE!

These peanut bugs are resting on a tree trunk. They have dull coloration, which helps them go unnoticed by hungry birds. But the lower peanut bug has been spotted. Suddenly it snaps open its wings to flash two huge spots that look like staring eyes. If the bug is lucky, the hungry bird will be startled into leaving it alone.

DOUBLE-DUTY CAMOUFLAGE

A Peruvian lichen mantis waits, almost invisible against the bark of a tree. Its camouflage disguises it from predators and also keeps its prey from seeing it—until it's too late.

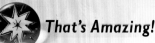

Word Builders

• **Camouflage**, from the French word *camoufler*, "to disguise," lets an animal blend into its surroundings. Insects have patterns and colors to hide against plants, pebbles, or dirt.
• **Mimic** is from the ancient Greek *mimos*, meaning "actor." To mimic is to copy or imitate something. Insects do this to fool their attackers into thinking they are dangerous or poisonous.

That's Amazing!

Since its enemies cannot see warning colors at night, the foul-tasting tiger moth has evolved a different way of letting predators, such as bats, know to beware. It has an organ underneath its thorax that produces sound when it flies, making a distinctive warning call that it tastes bad. Some tasty moths mimic this sound, too.

Pathfinder

• Peanut bugs are true bugs, just like cicadas and aphids. Find out what they have in common on pages 18–19.
• A spider that mimics a bird dropping? Read more about it on page 61.

LINES OF DEFENSE

KATYDID CONFUSION

This photo, right, is actually a katydid (a grasshopper cousin), but it has completely transformed itself by opening its wings. The move is enough to shock or confuse most predators and gives the katydid a chance to make a quick getaway.

BAD BLOOD

When disturbed, the bloody-nosed beetle breaks thin membranes in its mouth and forces out a droplet of its own blood. The blood has chemicals that will make its attacker very sick.

TAKE THAT!

When a wasp, bee, or ant wants to get rid of an attacker or immobilize prey, it uses a fearful weapon. The sting of a common wasp is painful, but it's nothing compared to that of a tarantula-hawk wasp or velvet ant, which can be agonizing. Some ants, such as the 24-hour ant from South America, have stings that burn like fire.

TOXIC SQUIRT

A bombardier beetle that's under attack will secrete chemicals into a chamber in its abdomen. They combine and react, making a hot substance that squirts out of the beetle.

TRUE COLORS

The monarch butterfly (right) is poisonous, as its bold orange colors warn. The viceroy (left) is harmless, but it mimics the monarch so predators will think it, too, is trouble— and will keep away.

SUIT OF ARMOR

All 6 inches (15 cm) of the Malaysian jungle nymph are covered in needle-sharp spines. If that doesn't put off an enemy, it makes a loud, rasping sound and waves its strong, spiny legs before slashing at any persistent attacker.

INSIDE STORY

Tastes Like Chicken?

Birds, frogs, snakes, and other arthropods aren't the only creatures that think insects make tasty treats. Many humans around the world also eat insects, which are an especially important source of protein in areas where people don't farm large animals for meat. Native Australians, for instance, eat sweet-tasting honeypot ants as well as meaty bogong moths—and the fat witchetty grubs shown at right. The witchetty grub is a caterpillar that lives in the roots of certain trees and tastes a little like unsalted peanut butter. In Africa, people collect thousands of tiny midges and make them into burgers. There are plans in China to use minced maggots as a substitute for beef and other meats. And chocolate-coated ants, first eaten in the Americas hundreds of years ago, are now snacked on all over the world.

Blister beetle　　　*Stink bug*

Beech-leaf roller case

Bagworm caterpillar case

Home, Sweet Home

HOME MEANS DIFFERENT things to different insects. For some, it's just the underside of a leaf that provides a spot to lay eggs on, or a simple resting place. But many insects go to more trouble, creating structures where their young can eat and grow in relative safety. Solitary bees and wasps may dig burrows or find holes in wood. Many larvae make their own protective apartments to hole up in out of leaves or debris. This way they can pass through their pupal stages in peace. Then there are the insects whose nests are among the most complex in the animal world. Termite mounds, for instance, are rock-solid structures that can be taller than an elephant and hold several million individuals. Scientists think some mounds may have been used for more than 4,000 years!

Insects build their homes from all kinds of materials. Ants mix soil with their own saliva to make a type of cement just right for underground tunneling. Termites add droppings…to make their cement extra-strong. Honeybees produce their building materials differently, secreting wax from a special gland in their abdomens. They use the wax to make the combs where they keep honey and young. Social wasps live in paper houses. They gnaw off wood, chew it into a paste, then work the paste into thin sheets of paper with their jaws. The many layers of paper they use act as insulation, protecting their delicate young in most kinds of weather.

THE TIES THAT BIND
These green tree ants wrestle the edges of two leaves together, preparing their new home to be sewn up with silk from their larvae. Other workers hold the larvae in their jaws and squeeze gently. The larvae dribble out a thin strand of silk—the thread that sews the leaves together. The tree house gets built, but some larvae may die from exhaustion.

Ventilation shaft

INSIDE STORY

The First Papermakers

Legend has it that the inventor of paper, Ts'ai Lun (AD 89–106) of China, learned how to make paper by watching wasps at work. He saw the way wasps used their powerful jaws to chew up wood fibers, mix it with their saliva, and make a paste. They then molded the paste into thin pieces and allowed it to dry. It hardened into paper but it was rather brittle and fell apart if crumpled. Ts'ai Lun perfected the wasp's art of papermaking by using glue instead of saliva and making long flat sheets in one pressing.

KEEP IT COOL
Cathedral termites in northern Australia call this huge, hard-as-concrete mound home. It can get very hot in this part of the world, but the mound acts like a cooling tower to keep the nest from overheating. Tunnels on the inside work the same as air-conditioning, letting the heat from the termites escape, while cooler air is sucked in from the ground below.

Potter wasp nest

Caddis fly larva case

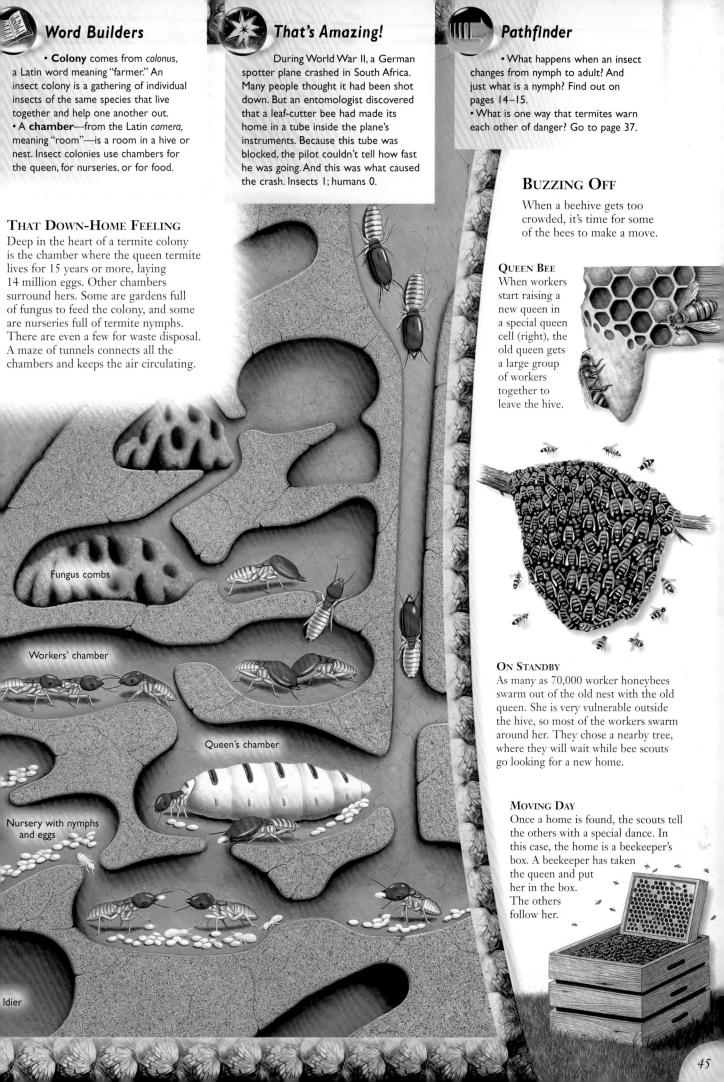

Word Builders

• **Colony** comes from *colonus*, a Latin word meaning "farmer." An insect colony is a gathering of individual insects of the same species that live together and help one another out.
• A **chamber**—from the Latin *camera*, meaning "room"—is a room in a hive or nest. Insect colonies use chambers for the queen, for nurseries, or for food.

That's Amazing!

During World War II, a German spotter plane crashed in South Africa. Many people thought it had been shot down. But an entomologist discovered that a leaf-cutter bee had made its home in a tube inside the plane's instruments. Because this tube was blocked, the pilot couldn't tell how fast he was going. And this was what caused the crash. Insects 1; humans 0.

Pathfinder

• What happens when an insect changes from nymph to adult? And just what is a nymph? Find out on pages 14–15.
• What is one way that termites warn each other of danger? Go to page 37.

THAT DOWN-HOME FEELING

Deep in the heart of a termite colony is the chamber where the queen termite lives for 15 years or more, laying 14 million eggs. Other chambers surround hers. Some are gardens full of fungus to feed the colony, and some are nurseries full of termite nymphs. There are even a few for waste disposal. A maze of tunnels connects all the chambers and keeps the air circulating.

Fungus combs

Workers' chamber

Queen's chamber

Nursery with nymphs and eggs

ldier

BUZZING OFF

When a beehive gets too crowded, it's time for some of the bees to make a move.

QUEEN BEE
When workers start raising a new queen in a special queen cell (right), the old queen gets a large group of workers together to leave the hive.

ON STANDBY
As many as 70,000 worker honeybees swarm out of the old nest with the old queen. She is very vulnerable outside the hive, so most of the workers swarm around her. They chose a nearby tree, where they will wait while bee scouts go looking for a new home.

MOVING DAY
Once a home is found, the scouts tell the others with a special dance. In this case, the home is a beekeeper's box. A beekeeper has taken the queen and put her in the box. The others follow her.

page **48** Is this a spider? Learn what to look for to make an identification.

Go to SPIDER VERSUS INSECT.

Spider Story

THESE CREATURES HAVE eight legs, but they are constantly mistaken for insects. What are they? They're spiders—and without them we'd be swimming in a virtual sea of insects. How have these amazing animals turned a talent for making silk thread into one of the most successful hunting and trapping tools? You are about to find out—you're going for a spin.

page **50** Some spiders come in strange shapes. Why is that?

Go to CLOSING IN.

page **52** This spider has huge eyes? Does this mean it has good eyesight?

Go to BODY LANGUAGE.

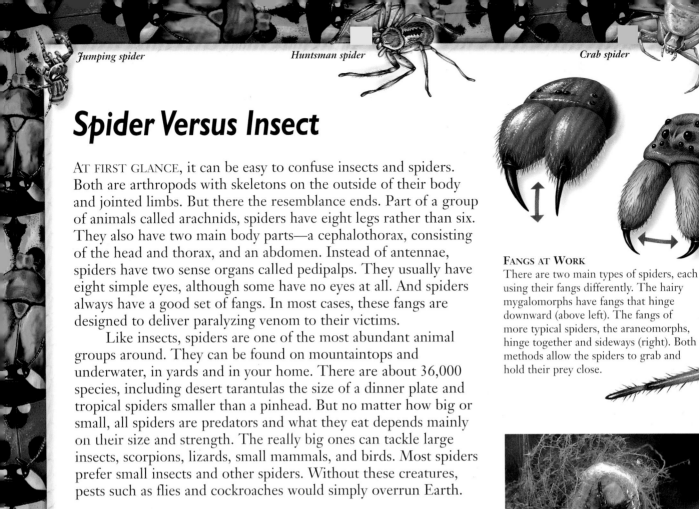

Spider Versus Insect

AT FIRST GLANCE, it can be easy to confuse insects and spiders. Both are arthropods with skeletons on the outside of their body and jointed limbs. But there the resemblance ends. Part of a group of animals called arachnids, spiders have eight legs rather than six. They also have two main body parts—a cephalothorax, consisting of the head and thorax, and an abdomen. Instead of antennae, spiders have two sense organs called pedipalps. They usually have eight simple eyes, although some have no eyes at all. And spiders always have a good set of fangs. In most cases, these fangs are designed to deliver paralyzing venom to their victims.

Like insects, spiders are one of the most abundant animal groups around. They can be found on mountaintops and underwater, in yards and in your home. There are about 36,000 species, including desert tarantulas the size of a dinner plate and tropical spiders smaller than a pinhead. But no matter how big or small, all spiders are predators and what they eat depends mainly on their size and strength. The really big ones can tackle large insects, scorpions, lizards, small mammals, and birds. Most spiders prefer small insects and other spiders. Without these creatures, pests such as flies and cockroaches would simply overrun Earth.

FANGS AT WORK
There are two main types of spiders, each using their fangs differently. The hairy mygalomorphs have fangs that hinge downward (above left). The fangs of more typical spiders, the araneomorphs, hinge together and sideways (right). Both methods allow the spiders to grab and hold their prey close.

INSIDE STORY

Spider People

Scientists who study spiders are called arachnologists. Some work with extremely dangerous spiders, carefully collecting venom to help make cures for a spider's toxic bite or to develop medicines for illnesses such as cancer and heart disease. Others study spider silk and have come up with ways to use it, such as making incredibly fine thread for sewing up wounds or better protective clothing like bulletproof vests. Conservation is another area where arachnologists are hard at work. As more natural habitats are destroyed, hundreds of spider species are in danger of becoming extinct. Many rare spiders are now bred in captivity so they can be released into the wild when their habitats are safe again.

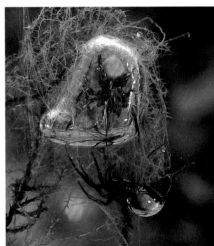

DIVING BELL
This aquatic spider lives underwater. To be able to breathe down there, it builds a diving bell out of silk and fills it with bubbles of air from the surface. It stays inside the bell during the day, leaving only at night to find food.

SPIDER WANNABES

Some arachnids look a lot like spiders, but don't let them fool you.

CHECK OUT THOSE SEGMENTS
A solpugid might look like a hairy spider, but it has the segmented abdomen that is common in scorpions. Solpugids have the most powerful jaws, in proportion to size, of any animal. They slice up mice, birds, and lizards into a pulp, then eat the pieces.

Word Builders

In an ancient Greek myth, Arachne was a woman who challenged the goddess Athena to a weaving contest. This angered Athena, so she decided to change Arachne into a spider who would have to weave forever. The **arachnids**—including spiders—are named for her.

That's Amazing!

The first time you see a black widow or redback spider, it's hard to believe that something so small can be so dangerous. In fact, these pea-size spiders can inject a venom that is 15 times more toxic than that of a rattlesnake. Fortunately, they are shy creatures and prefer to hide.

Pathfinder

• How does a spider survive if it can't see very well? Go to pages 52–53.
• Molting is one of the most dangerous moments in a spider's life. Find out why on pages 54–55.
• A spider that spits? Stand back and flip to page 58 to see it in action.

Eye
Some spiders have excellent eyesight. Others are blind.

Abdomen
This contains the silk-making glands, lungs, and other vital organs.

Pedipalp
The pedipalps, or palps, are used as sense organs or to manipulate food. Males also use them to transfer sperm during mating.

Chelicera
Two fangs are attached to the chelicerae, or jaws. In most species, they contain venom ducts.

Claw
Many spiders have toothed claws plus hairs that help grip their webs.

GOOD-GUY SPIDER

This marbled orb weaver isn't a danger to humans. In fact, it's a big help. It will eat more than 350 flies and wasps in its lifetime, getting rid of some pesky insects. Despite their bad reputation, spiders are valuable natural pest controllers, helping to limit populations of cockroaches, flies, and even scorpions.

Cephalothorax
This includes the head and thorax, and also has the jaws and legs attached to it.

Leg
All spiders have eight jointed legs. The back legs sometimes have special claws to wrap prey in silk.

TARANTULA TIMES TWO

Spiders have exoskeletons, so they have to molt to get bigger, just like insects. This red-kneed tarantula has just wriggled out of its old exoskeleton (left).

COUNT THE BODY PARTS

Mites appear to have one body part, but they actually have two. Most are microscopic, but this red velvet mite is large enough to see unaided. Mites are found almost anywhere—from the nostrils of seals to the "ears" of moths—and there are probably more of them on Earth than any other arthropod.

LOOK PAST THE LEGS

Although this harvestman— or daddy long legs as it is also called—looks a lot like a spider, it appears to have only one body section, much like mites. Despite their name, some in this group have short legs.

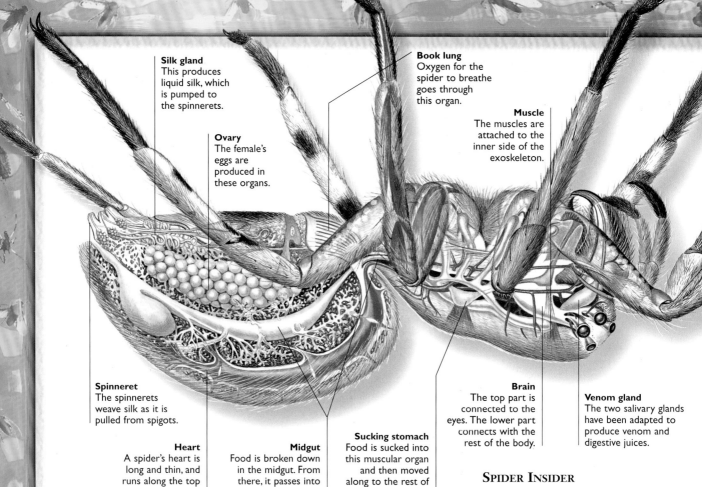

Silk gland
This produces liquid silk, which is pumped to the spinnerets.

Ovary
The female's eggs are produced in these organs.

Book lung
Oxygen for the spider to breathe goes through this organ.

Muscle
The muscles are attached to the inner side of the exoskeleton.

Spinneret
The spinnerets weave silk as it is pulled from spigots.

Heart
A spider's heart is long and thin, and runs along the top of the abdomen.

Midgut
Food is broken down in the midgut. From there, it passes into the bloodstream.

Sucking stomach
Food is sucked into this muscular organ and then moved along to the rest of the digestive tract.

Brain
The top part is connected to the eyes. The lower part connects with the rest of the body.

Venom gland
The two salivary glands have been adapted to produce venom and digestive juices.

SPIDER INSIDER
To get a clearer idea of how a spider functions, take a look inside the body of a brown badge huntsman. This fast-moving predator, with a telltale dark-brown patch on the cephalothorax, is a typical spider.

Closing In

A QUICK LOOK inside a spider's body shows that it has a number of body systems in common with other animals. It has a brain, which is the body's main control center. It has a heart that pumps nutrient-rich blood to vital organs. It has lungs for breathing air. And it has a system for breaking down food into usable nutrients. As with insects, though, these systems work a little differently than in vertebrates.

Most spiders actually have two ways to get oxygen. Air filters through slits in the abdomen into the book lung chambers, where it seeps into the blood and is then carried to the body parts. Many species also have a few tracheae, or breathing tubes, that are connected to breathing holes, just as insects have. Some spiders have no tracheae and two sets of book lungs.

The only way spiders can eat is to slurp up fluids. So, while some have mouthparts that can mash prey, all spiders must partly digest, or liquefy, their food before they can eat it. Most inject paralyzing venom into their prey, and then spit digestive juices into the victim to dissolve the tissues. The liquid results are vacuumed up by the sucking stomach into the digestive tract.

Another important body system is not exactly unique to spiders. Other arthropod species make silk, but only spiders have perfected the system and to such deadly effect.

SPIGOTS AND SILKS
Special glands inside a spider's abdomen make liquid silk. This is secreted to the spider's spinnerets, where it is pulled out of hairlike cones called spigots, magnified here 170 times. Spiders have between one and three pairs of spinnerets, and each spinneret has different types of spigots for different types of silk.

Tarantula

Lynx spider

That's Amazing!

Most spiders live only 2 to 3 years, unless they're one of the large tropical tarantulas. Most of these tarantulas live 7 to 15 years, but one exception is the Mexican red-kneed tarantula—it can take almost 7 years to become an adult. For the males, that's almost the end of their lives and most die 6 to 12 months later. However, the females can live more than 30 years.

- Insect innards work a bit differently from a spider's. Find out about insect systems on pages 10–11.
- Learn how spiders keep from getting stuck in their own silk webs on page 56.

ODD ARACHNIDS

SPINES AND SHARP PARTS
Some spiders do not come in the standard spider shape. Scientists don't know why the curved spined spider (right) looks the way it does, but there's good reason for the arrow-shaped spiny orb weaver (below) to have sharp protrusions that stick out from its abdomen. They make it very unpleasant for a small bird to swallow.

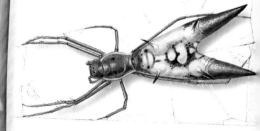

BELLY-UP
The underside of this common garden spider, seen hanging from its web, provides a very different view of a spider. You can see its fangs folded into their grooves in the chelicerae, and where its legs join the cephalothorax. The spinnerets are also visible on the tip of the abdomen.

BREAK UP
The peculiar knob on the wheel web spider's abdomen breaks up the pattern of its body, making it difficult for a predator to see.

HANDS ON

Spider Watching: Part 1

Most spiders are very secretive and like to hide out. But no matter where you look, there's bound to be a spider lurking nearby.

❶ Never touch a spider unless you know it is completely harmless. Few species are dangerous, but many can give painful nips.

❷ Never put your fingers where you cannot see them, whether it's inside a hole or under a log or rock.

❸ It's a good idea to take an adult along for advice.

❹ Indoors: Look for orb weavers on window-sills. They'll be in the middle of their webs or tucked up in a corner of the window.

❺ Dark, dry attics (right): When you find a house spider web, tap it very gently. The spider should scuttle out to see if it has food.

❻ Outdoors: Spiders may be tricky to find—they tend to hide under stones or pieces of wood.

THE HIGH VIEW
This minute spider has eyes high up on its cephalothorax. Some scientists think this helps it spot prey. Others think the long jaws may help in grabbing food.

LONG AND THIN
With its narrow body, the long-jawed orb weaver can hide from predators by lying flat along a grass stem.

Trapdoor spider   *Comb-footed spider*

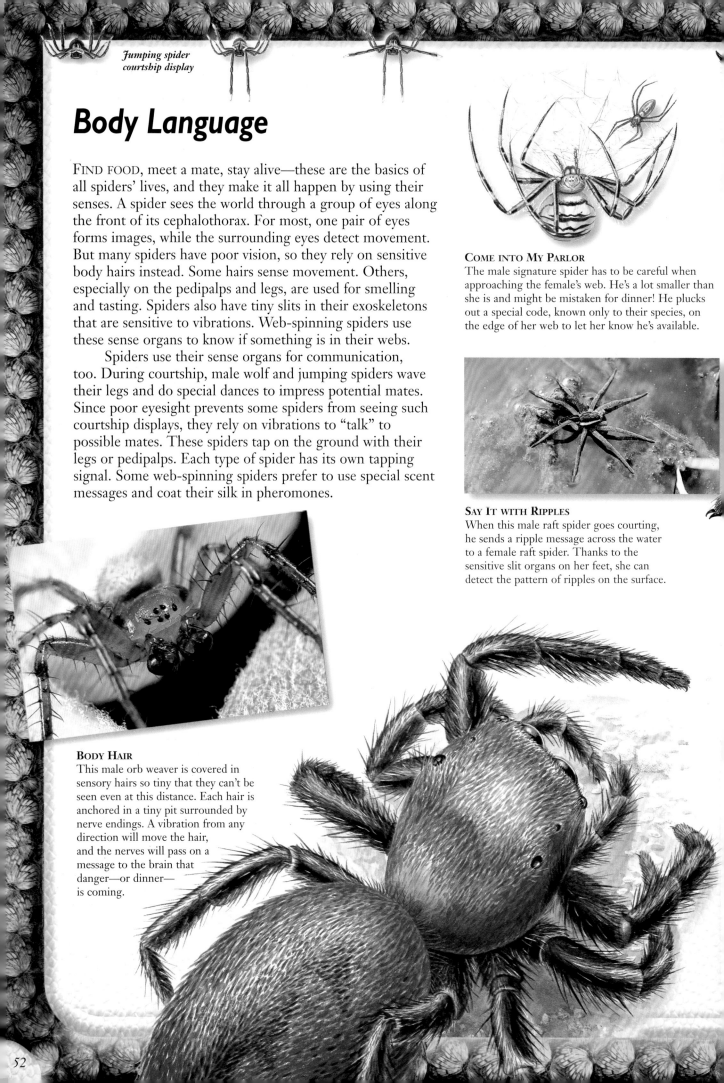

Jumping spider courtship display

Body Language

FIND FOOD, meet a mate, stay alive—these are the basics of all spiders' lives, and they make it all happen by using their senses. A spider sees the world through a group of eyes along the front of its cephalothorax. For most, one pair of eyes forms images, while the surrounding eyes detect movement. But many spiders have poor vision, so they rely on sensitive body hairs instead. Some hairs sense movement. Others, especially on the pedipalps and legs, are used for smelling and tasting. Spiders also have tiny slits in their exoskeletons that are sensitive to vibrations. Web-spinning spiders use these sense organs to know if something is in their webs.

Spiders use their sense organs for communication, too. During courtship, male wolf and jumping spiders wave their legs and do special dances to impress potential mates. Since poor eyesight prevents some spiders from seeing such courtship displays, they rely on vibrations to "talk" to possible mates. These spiders tap on the ground with their legs or pedipalps. Each type of spider has its own tapping signal. Some web-spinning spiders prefer to use special scent messages and coat their silk in pheromones.

COME INTO MY PARLOR
The male signature spider has to be careful when approaching the female's web. He's a lot smaller than she is and might be mistaken for dinner! He plucks out a special code, known only to their species, on the edge of her web to let her know he's available.

SAY IT WITH RIPPLES
When this male raft spider goes courting, he sends a ripple message across the water to a female raft spider. Thanks to the sensitive slit organs on her feet, she can detect the pattern of ripples on the surface.

BODY HAIR
This male orb weaver is covered in sensory hairs so tiny that they can't be seen even at this distance. Each hair is anchored in a tiny pit surrounded by nerve endings. A vibration from any direction will move the hair, and the nerves will pass on a message to the brain that danger—or dinner—is coming.

Word Builders

Dandy jumper aside (see below), almost all spider and insect behavior is instinctive. **Instinctive behavior** is behavior passed on via genes. For example, a human baby will automatically hold her breath when underwater. Learned behavior is different—a baby has to learn not to touch a hot oven, by being told or getting burned.

That's Amazing!

A female spider usually eats her mate only if he's clumsy or if she gets distracted. Not so with the six-humped dome spider. The tiny male must leap and grab hold of the female. But he can't hold on and mate at the same time. To keep him from falling off, the female buries her fangs in him, then consumes his bodily fluids.

Pathfinder

• Find out about the multipurpose sense organ that insects have but spiders don't on pages 12–13.
• What does it usually mean when a spider's web gets disturbed? Go to pages 56–57.

EYES OF THE SPIDER

To understand how a spider lives and how it gets its food, take a look at its eyes.

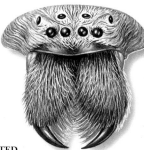

FARSIGHTED
As its name suggests, the huntsman spider actively hunts its food. The huntsman's eyes are spread out to give it fairly good all-around vision for spotting prey.

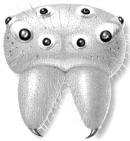

SIT AND WAIT
The crab spider's super vibration sensors help it detect prey from a distance. Its keen vision kicks in as the prey nears.

SIX EYES
The woodlouse-eating spider has six very small eyes instead of eight. This nighthunter uses its sense of touch to uncover prey under stones and bark.

NIGHT VISION
The ogre-faced spider has two huge eyes that are hundreds of times more sensitive to light than human eyes. It can see prey in near total darkness.

SHALL WE DANCE?
This male jumping spider has spotted a female. Immediately he'll start waving his front legs in the air to show off his colors and patterns, which are unique to his species and help the female recognize him as a potential mate. Once he gets her attention, he'll sashay up to her in a zigzag maneuver and gently stroke her. If she's interested, the two will mate.

INSIDE STORY

Smart Spider

Most spiders use the same hunting method, no matter what kind of prey they're pursuing. This is called instinctive behavior. But the dandy jumper changes the way it hunts depending on the type of spider it is hunting. When it comes across a new web, it taps gently, pretending to be a courting male tapping out a greeting. After trial and error, it taps out the correct message, and the female spider comes over to meet her mate—but gets gobbled up instead. The dandy jumper memorizes the message for use in the future whenever it comes across the same type of web.

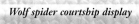

Wolf spider courtship display

A Spider's Life

FEMALE SPIDERS LAY their eggs within a few weeks of mating. Some spiders produce a few eggs at a time, but others can lay 1,000 or more. All spider mothers wrap up their eggs in silk to keep them moist and safe from parasites. Many mothers die soon after laying their eggs, leaving the babies to hatch on their own. But trapdoor spiders guard their eggs in their burrows, while wolf spiders and nursery-web spiders carry their egg sacs everywhere until hatching time several months later.

Hatching babies must first break out of their eggs, then fight their way out of the egg sac. They don't eat for the first few days, living instead off the last of their yolk sac, and usually stay clustered together. Some spiderlings have mothers that protect and feed them—the window lace-weaver spider even sacrifices herself as her babies' first meal! But most have to fend for themselves. Once they start to grow, they must leave the nest, or they'll start eating one another. They either scuttle off or balloon away to find themselves a good spot for a new home. Like all arthropods, spider young must shed their old exoskeletons in order to grow. Depending on the species, a spider can molt six to 30 times during its life.

SPIDER SPOUSES
Spiders mate in many different ways. The female green lynx spider is on the left. The female will attach a line of silk to the leaf on which she is standing, then leap into the air. The male will follow her on his line of silk, so they can mate in midair, hanging from their draglines.

PIGGYBACK
This female wolf spider carried her egg sac on her spinnerets for weeks. She cut open the egg sac to help her young during hatching, and now she's giving her spiderlings a ride. They'll stay with her until their first molt. Then they're on their own.

HANDS ON

Spider Watching: Part 2

WARNING: If you live near poisonous spiders, do not attempt this activity. The best thing to take with you on a spider hunt is a clear plastic container. Place the bottom section of the plastic container over the spider, being careful to avoid trapping its legs—remember that spiders, with their long legs and soft bodies, are very easy to injure or even squash and kill if you handle them roughly. Slowly drag the container back over the lid. Close it up and the spider will be inside, ready for inspection with a magnifying glass. Once you have finished, let the spider go where you found it.

You can also examine the molted skins of spiders. They are very fragile, so use tweezers to pick them up carefully, and a magnifying glass to get a closer look.

THE SPIDER'S NEW CLOTHES

Shedding skin is hard to do—and dangerous! If the weather is too dry, for instance, a spider can get stuck in its old exoskeleton and die. The new exoskeleton can stay soft for more than a day, leaving the spider especially vulnerable to attack. Males usually stop molting when they reach adulthood.

SPLIT START
A female giant wood spider hangs from her web as her old exoskeleton splits along the edge of her cephalothorax.

BIG BREAK
The old skin covering her abdomen tears apart and starts to come away as she tries to pull her legs free.

Word Builders

• Baby spiders are called **spiderlings**. After molting a few times, spiders are called **juveniles**, and when almost identical to adults, **sub-adults**.
• **Ballooning** is used by juvenile and small adult spiders for long-distance travel. Spiders make a long strand of silk that catches the wind and lifts them into the air, to be carried where the wind takes them, like hot-air ballooning.

That's Amazing!

• After the huge volcanic explosion of the island of Krakatau in 1883, every living thing was wiped out. However, in just a few months, animals started appearing again. The very first arrival was a ballooning spider.
• A New Zealand spider species lives in freezing coastal waters. The nest, which the female shares with her babies for five months, is attached to seaweed.

Pathfinder

• Like spiders, insects molt to grow. Find out how they do it on pages 14–15.
• Learn what spiders like to eat—apart from one another—on pages 58–59.
• Could a spider survive if it lost a leg? Go to page 61.

MOTHER ON CALL

There's a good reason for calling this creature "the nursery-web spider." She carries her egg sac wherever she goes, and once her babies are ready to hatch, she builds them a special nursery area out of silk. She'll even stand guard over the young and chase off small predators that get too close.

LEGS OUT

The spider pulls her long, fragile legs clear of the old skin very slowly. It's like taking off a glove, but if anything goes wrong, she could end up without her new legs.

DOUBLE DANGLE

Finally free, the giant wood spider dangles helplessly from the old exoskeleton as blood pumps around her body, expanding her new exoskeleton while it is still soft. She won't be able to climb back into the web until it hardens after about 20 minutes.

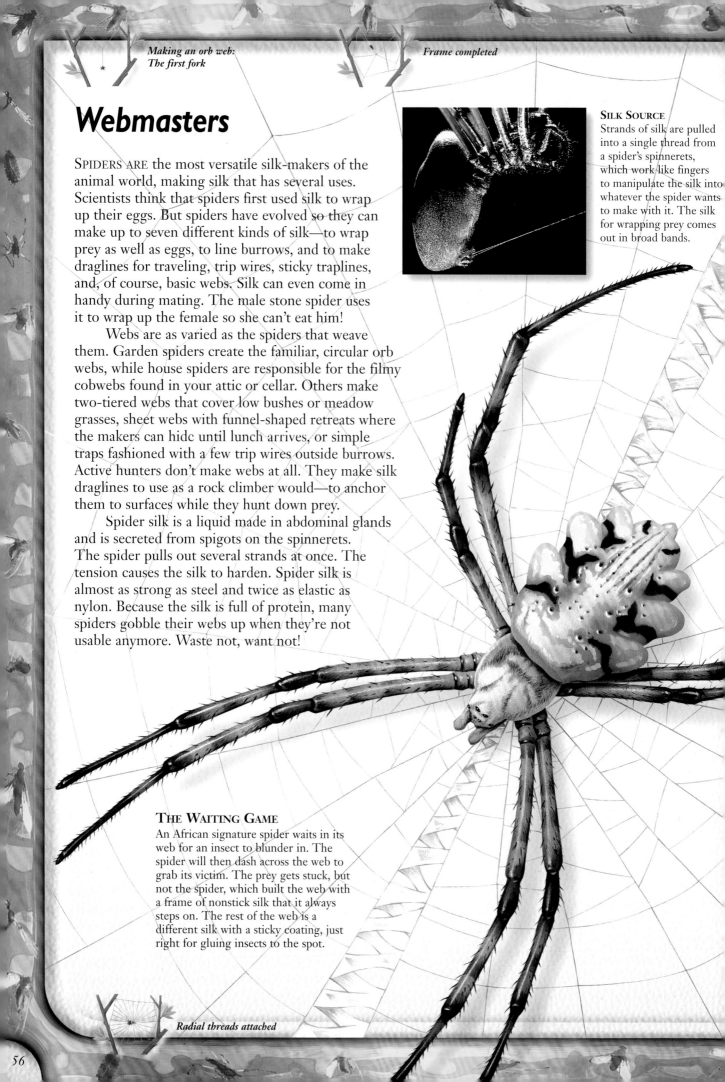

Webmasters

SPIDERS ARE the most versatile silk-makers of the animal world, making silk that has several uses. Scientists think that spiders first used silk to wrap up their eggs. But spiders have evolved so they can make up to seven different kinds of silk—to wrap prey as well as eggs, to line burrows, and to make draglines for traveling, trip wires, sticky traplines, and, of course, basic webs. Silk can even come in handy during mating. The male stone spider uses it to wrap up the female so she can't eat him!

Webs are as varied as the spiders that weave them. Garden spiders create the familiar, circular orb webs, while house spiders are responsible for the filmy cobwebs found in your attic or cellar. Others make two-tiered webs that cover low bushes or meadow grasses, sheet webs with funnel-shaped retreats where the makers can hide until lunch arrives, or simple traps fashioned with a few trip wires outside burrows. Active hunters don't make webs at all. They make silk draglines to use as a rock climber would—to anchor them to surfaces while they hunt down prey.

Spider silk is a liquid made in abdominal glands and is secreted from spigots on the spinnerets. The spider pulls out several strands at once. The tension causes the silk to harden. Spider silk is almost as strong as steel and twice as elastic as nylon. Because the silk is full of protein, many spiders gobble their webs up when they're not usable anymore. Waste not, want not!

SILK SOURCE

Strands of silk are pulled into a single thread from a spider's spinnerets, which work like fingers to manipulate the silk into whatever the spider wants to make with it. The silk for wrapping prey comes out in broad bands.

THE WAITING GAME

An African signature spider waits in its web for an insect to blunder in. The spider will then dash across the web to grab its victim. The prey gets stuck, but not the spider, which built the web with a frame of nonstick silk that it always steps on. The rest of the web is a different silk with a sticky coating, just right for gluing insects to the spot.

Radial threads attached

Word Builders

- The word **spider** comes from the Old English word *spinnan*, "to spin."
- **Secretion** is the process whereby a plant or animal releases a special substance. Spiders secrete silk from silk glands, while humans secrete tears from tear glands.
- **Ultraviolet light** is at the far end of the light spectrum. Humans cannot see it, but spiders and insects can.

That's Amazing!

Some giant orb-weaving spiders from tropical countries make webs that are so strong they can catch small birds in them. In Papua New Guinea, where the largest of these spiders are found, the local people use giant wood spiders' webs, which are 9 feet (2.7 m) across, as fishing nets.

Pathfinder

- What does a bee see when it looks at a flower? Find out on page 12.
- Silk clothing is made from insect spit. Say what? Learn more on page 23.

WEB DESIGN

The way a web looks depends on the spider that has spun it. Spiderwebs range from careful constructions to tangled masses. Some spiders make a new web every night. Others just do repairs, spinning a new web only if they really have to because the old web has lost its stickiness.

HAMMOCK WEB
The hammock web spun by a money spider over low bushes may look messy, but any insect caught in its fine lattice weave usually falls into another web suspended below.

LACE-SHEET WEB
The trap spun by a lace-web weaver is made of fine, woolly silk. It may not be sticky, but insects soon get tangled up in it.

SCAFFOLD WEB
A scaffold web has stretched traplines with sticky ends attached to the ground. If a crawling insect walks into a trapline, the line snaps back, with the victim dangling in the air.

TRIANGLE WEB
The triangle spider holds its web in its front legs while anchored by a thread to the twig behind it. When an insect hits the web, the spider releases it and the web collapses, entangling the prey.

TOUCHY TRIP-UP
Having spread a series of silken trip wires in front of its silk-lined burrow, this funnel-web spider sits and waits. When an insect walks across a trip wire, the spider will feel the vibrations—and strike.

TRAP AND WRAP
This garden spider moves fast to wrap up dinner. But the insect trapped in its web is a wasp, so it must first immobilize the struggling wasp in a straitjacket of silk. That keeps the wasp from stinging. Only then will the spider inject its venom.

The Visible Web

Insects can see webs because they can see ultraviolet light, which webs reflect. So why don't they fly around them? Scientists think that some webs look like the ultraviolet patterns made by flowers. Butterflies and bees think they're flying toward flowers full of nectar instead of a sticky web. Other webs may appear as a bright source of light and attract moths the way candles do. Signature spiders often strengthen the center of their webs with zigzag patterns called stabilimenta. Each species has its own pattern—perhaps to lure insects or to act as a visual warning to birds (and humans!) to detour. The stabilimenta may give the spider shade from the hot sun, like an umbrella, or a safe place to molt.

Scaffold spiral of dry silk in place

Spiral of sticky silk added

Spiders Stalking

ALL SPIDERS are meat-eaters. While most are trappers, there are 18,000 species that no longer use silk webs to ensnare prey. These are spiders that actively hunt for food or wait in ambush for it.

Spiders that hunt stake out their own territory. Some wolf spiders will chase off any intruder that tries to move in on their turf. Jumping spiders are more free roaming and can often be seen close to each other, leaping after prey with silk draglines sailing out behind them. Bolas spiders use silk to hunt with, but not to make webs. They actually go fishing for their prey, casting out a silken thread with a sticky blob at the end to reel in flying insects. Most hunters eat ants, beetles, and other spiders, but larger individuals—like some tarantulas and huntsmen—can sometimes snag lizards, frogs, rodents, fish, and even birds.

Ambushers wait quietly until lunch comes close enough for them to grab. Trapdoor spiders wait in their tunnels, just beneath trapdoors made from silk, ready to rush out the second they detect vibrations caused by prey. Others simply blend in with the flowers, leaves, or bark of their surroundings, biding their time until some unsuspecting insect wanders within range.

ANYONE HOME?
A trapdoor spider pushes up its trapdoor of soil and silk, thus revealing its presence. But when the spider is inside with the door shut, you wouldn't know it was there. The hinged trapdoor blends in perfectly with the ground.

SPITTING DISTANCE
This spitting spider is too slow to actually catch a fly, so it delivers its paralyzing venom from a distance. When it gets within a body length of its victim, it shoots streams of sticky venom from its venom glands all over the fly, which roots it to the spot.

INSIDE STORY

Tale of the Tarantula

The large European wolf spider, *Lycosa narbonensis*, was the original tarantula. It got this name because it lived around Taranto, a town in southern Italy. During the 14th century, lots of people were suddenly bitten by spiders, and these tarantulas got the blame. People thought that if they danced wildly until they collapsed from exhaustion, they would not die from the tarantula's bite. This became known as "tarantism," and the dance and music it inspired were called the tarantella. But the relatively harmless European wolf spider wasn't the problem—it was almost certainly the European black widow spider. When Europeans moved to the Americas, they called the large hairy spiders there "tarantulas." Now "tarantula" refers to these New World spiders only.

THE POISON PACK
Out of the 35,000 known species of spiders, only 30 have venom that is really harmful to humans. Some of these are vigorous ambushers or hunters, but others are quiet web-spinners. And most live in areas of tropical countries where very few people live. There are medicines, called antivenins, to offset spiders' venom, so most people survive their bites.

VIOLIN SPIDER
The venom of the violin spider rarely kills people, but it can destroy flesh. A single bite can eat into the skin and cause a wound 5 inches (12.7 cm) wide and more than 1 inch (2.5 cm) deep.

FUNNEL-WEB SPIDER
With its large fangs, potent venom, and aggressive attitude, the Sydney funnel-web spider is one to avoid. Male funnel-webs are the only male spiders with venomous bites that are dangerous to humans.

Word Builders

The **bolas spider** gets its name from a tool used by South American cowboys to trip up cattle. A *bolas* is a long rope with a weight attached to the ends. The scientists who gave the bolas spider its common name thought that its method of catching food looked similar to the way the herdsmen used their bolas.

That's Amazing!

Most spiders live alone, but one social spider species lives in huge colonies in the rain forests of Peru. The webs of a colony can cover 256 square feet (25 sq m) and be home to thousands of spiders. Although they are each no wider than 0.8 inch (2 cm), they can capture prey as large as small birds by working as a team.

Pathfinder

• Who's a better hunter—an insect or a spider? Turn to pages 34–35 to compare notes.
• Sneak a peek at a Mexican red-kneed tarantula just after it has molted on page 49.
• Find out why scientists collect venom from deadly spiders on page 61.

READY AND WAITING
As it's doing here in a cluster of white flowers, a crab spider can change its coloring to match surrounding flowers. The crab spider's venom is very toxic to insects, allowing this very small spider to kill bees twice its size.

TARANTULA ATTACK
This large Mexican red-kneed tarantula can either wait in its burrow for lunch to walk its way, or it can go out hunting. But it has very poor eyesight for a hunter, so it uses sense organs on its legs to pick up the vibrations made by a passing lizard. It rears up, ready to strike faster than the eye can see. Then it sinks its fangs—all 0.4 inch (1 cm) of them—into its victim. That's usually enough to make the kill. But this lizard is larger, so the tarantula might have to inject some venom to stop the struggling.

WANDERING SPIDER
The Brazilian wandering spider is one of the most dangerous spiders in the world. It is big and aggressive, with a fast-acting venom that can kill in 15 minutes. Luckily, it's not common in heavily populated cities.

BLACK WIDOW
The southern black widow is one of the most feared spiders in the world. Yet it is a small, shy spider that will only bite a human if it is provoked.

59

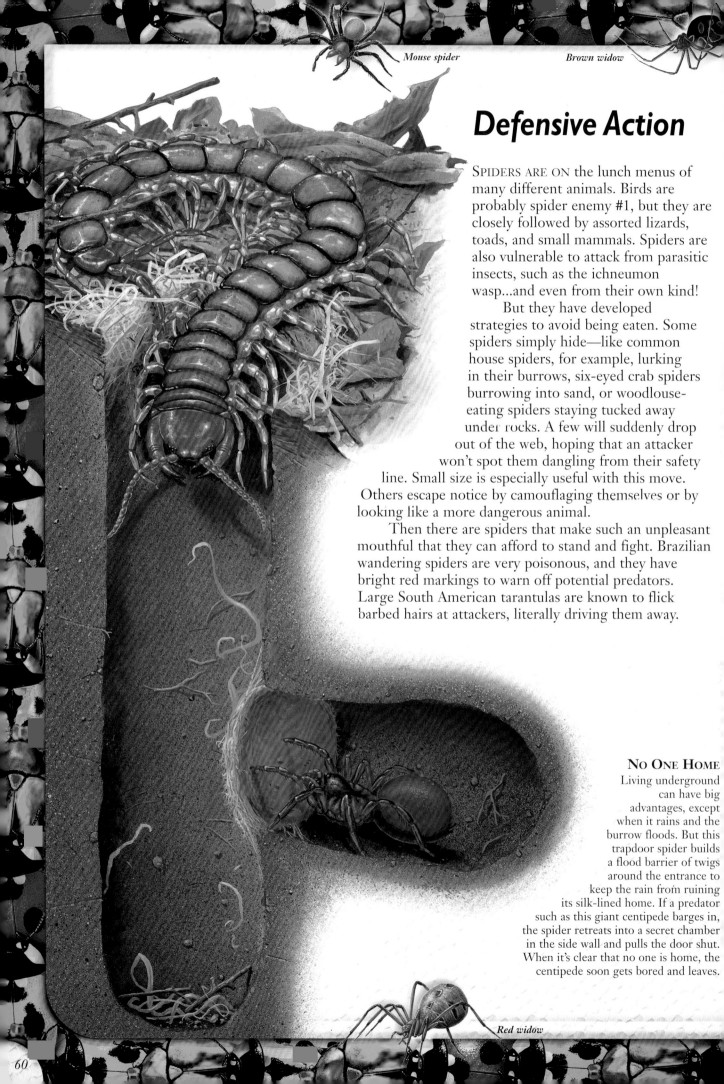

Defensive Action

SPIDERS ARE ON the lunch menus of many different animals. Birds are probably spider enemy #1, but they are closely followed by assorted lizards, toads, and small mammals. Spiders are also vulnerable to attack from parasitic insects, such as the ichneumon wasp...and even from their own kind!

But they have developed strategies to avoid being eaten. Some spiders simply hide—like common house spiders, for example, lurking in their burrows, six-eyed crab spiders burrowing into sand, or woodlouse-eating spiders staying tucked away under rocks. A few will suddenly drop out of the web, hoping that an attacker won't spot them dangling from their safety line. Small size is especially useful with this move. Others escape notice by camouflaging themselves or by looking like a more dangerous animal.

Then there are spiders that make such an unpleasant mouthful that they can afford to stand and fight. Brazilian wandering spiders are very poisonous, and they have bright red markings to warn off potential predators. Large South American tarantulas are known to flick barbed hairs at attackers, literally driving them away.

NO ONE HOME

Living underground can have big advantages, except when it rains and the burrow floods. But this trapdoor spider builds a flood barrier of twigs around the entrance to keep the rain from ruining its silk-lined home. If a predator such as this giant centipede barges in, the spider retreats into a secret chamber in the side wall and pulls the door shut. When it's clear that no one is home, the centipede soon gets bored and leaves.

Red widow

Word Builders

Antivenin is also known as antivenom. It is from the Latin words for "against poison." It is a substance that works against the effects of the bite or sting of a venomous creature. Each type of venomous spider requires its own antivenin. For example, a person bitten by a widow must be treated with widow antivenin.

That's Amazing!

Though large South American tarantulas have fearsome jaws, their venom is less than deadly. But the hairs on their abdomens have barbed ends. If a tarantula is disturbed, it brushes off clouds of these hairs at its attacker with quick kicks of its back legs. If the hairs get into the eyes or nose, the pain can stop the attacker in its tracks.

Pathfinder

• Find out how wasps lunch on tarantulas on page 35.
• How do insects use camouflage? Go to pages 42–43.
• Having an odd shape helps some spiders protect themselves. Learn more on page 51.

LOOK-ALIKES

DEAD-LEAF DISGUISE
A scorpion spider hangs in the air imitating a dried-up leaf. Why? Because no predator is going to want to eat a dead leaf. Other times, this spider curls the tip of its abdomen and resembles a dangerous scorpion.

HIDE AND SEEK
As long as she stays very still, it's unlikely that this female lichen spider will be seen. Predators are usually on the lookout for a spider's familiar shape, but her outline is almost invisible against the bark of a tree. Many spiders camouflage their egg sacs, too, with moss, leaves, and twigs.

ON A ROLL
When the South African white lady spider spots trouble, it's out of there! It curls its legs up under its body and rolls down sand dunes, cartwheeling out of danger at amazing speeds.

ANT ANTICS
Several spider species mimic ants, because predators stay away from ant bites and stings. But one Brazilian ant-mimicking spider uses its disguise to get up close to the ants it looks like—then eats them!

DUNG BY DAY
This female bird-dung spider spends her day pretending to be a bird dropping—not a popular food choice. But at night she releases a chemical that tricks male moths into thinking she's a female moth. When they arrive, she quickly gobbles them up.

SHORT A LEG
How many legs does this spider have? In a last-ditch attempt to escape a predator that had it by its eighth leg, this spider has shed the leg and run away. Many spiders will cut off their own legs in response to danger, and there is no limit as to how many legs they can lose and survive, as long as they manage to eat. The legs are often completely regrown if the spider has more molts to go through.

INSIDE STORY

Poison Protection

Up until the late 19th century, if you got bitten by a really venomous spider, there wasn't much that could be done to help you. Then scientists discovered how to create a cure, called antivenin. First, a sample of the venom must be collected. Scientists do this by giving a spider a small electric shock, which causes the venom glands to contract and squirt out the venom. Small amounts of the substance are then injected into a mammal, which develops antibodies that fight the venom's effects. These antibodies are removed from the animal's blood and injected into a spider-bite victim...and the cure begins.

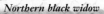
Northern black widow

Redback spider

WHICH WAY THE WASP?
Few predators will attack an Asian mutillid wasp because of its painful sting. So this jumping spider from Borneo has evolved into an almost perfect wasp mimic, but backwards. Its long, wiggly spinnerets look just like an insect's antennae.

Rove beetle

Huntsman spider chelicerae and fangs

Glossary

abdomen The rear part of an insect's or spider's body. It holds the organs of the digestive, respiratory, and reproductive systems, as well as the heart.

adaptation Changes an animal or plant makes to help it survive in a particular environment or under certain conditions. Crab spiders have developed the ability to change color to match the flower they are standing on as an adaptation to help them ambush prey.

antenna A delicate sense organ on an insect's head, which it uses to smell, touch, or hear the world. Insects have two antennae, which can be long or short, thin, branched, or featherlike.

arachnid An arthropod with eight legs. Spiders and their relatives—including ticks, mites, solpugids, and scorpions—are all arachnids.

arachnologist A scientist who studies spiders and their relatives.

arthropod An animal with jointed legs and a body divided into segments covered by an exoskeleton. The arthropods are an extremely varied group of animals that includes insects and spiders as well as crabs, scorpions, centipedes, millipedes, ticks, and mites.

ballooning A method used by spiderlings and small adult spiders to travel long distances. They are carried on the wind as they dangle from a long strand of silk.

camouflage Colors or patterns that help disguise an animal so that it blends with and remains hidden in its environment. Insects and spiders camouflage themselves as leaves, bark, or flowers to avoid being seen by predators or prey.

caste A social group that carries out certain tasks. Ants and social bees are divided into two main castes—the queen and the workers.

caterpillar The larva of a moth or butterfly.

cephalothorax The head and thorax of a spider combined in one body segment. The mouthparts, palps, and the eight legs are attached to it, and it also holds the spider's brain, venom glands, and sucking stomach.

chelicerae A spider's mouthparts, used for grabbing and sometimes crushing its prey. A sharp fang hinges from each chelicera, allowing most species to inject venom into prey, killing or paralyzing it.

chitin The light yet tough material that makes up an insect's exoskeleton and wings.

cocoon A protective case, usually made of silk. Insects such as moths, butterflies, some wasps, antlions, lacewings, and many others make cocoons to keep themselves safe while they go through the pupal stage and turn into adults.

colony A group of animals of the same species that live and work together to survive. The inhabitants of an ant nest, termite mound, and beehive are all examples of an insect colony.

complete metamorphosis One of two main ways in which an insect develops. It changes from an egg to a larva to a pupa to a mature insect adult. The larva looks very different from the adult, and the change in appearance is sudden, as can be witnessed in butterflies, moths, beetles, flies, bees, wasps, and ants.

compound eye An insect's main pair of eyes, made up of many smaller eyes, or lenses, each one of which sees movement separately.

dragline A line of silk that a spider will trail behind it as it moves around, occasionally attaching to surfaces. This allows the spider to hunt, find a mate, or drop out of its web suddenly, and always be able to find the way back home.

egg sac A silk covering woven by a female spider to wrap up her eggs, to protect them, and keep them from drying out.

elytra A beetle's forewings. These two wings are hard and provide a protective covering for the beetle's delicate pair of flying wings, which are underneath. They also keep the beetle stable when it is flying.

entomologist A scientist who studies insects.

evolution The gradual change that occurs in plants and animals over many years as they adapt to changing environments and conditions.

exoskeleton The hard, outer skeleton of an arthropod. It is a tough, jointed shell made of chitin, which supports the muscles and soft internal organs.

grub The larva of an ant, bee, wasp, or beetle. It can look a little like a caterpillar.

haltere One of a pair of knoblike structures. The halteres are the modified back wings of flies and allow them to keep their bodies balanced and level during flight.

hibernation The practice of remaining inactive during the cold winter months. Like bears, many insects hibernate, either as eggs, larvae, pupae, or adults.

invertebrate An animal that has no backbone. Some invertebrates, such as worms and jellyfish, have soft bodies, but others, like the arthropods, are protected by their hard exoskeletons.

larva The immature stage of insects that look completely different from their parents and undergo complete metamorphosis to become adults. Caterpillars, maggots, and grubs are all larvae.

maggot The legless larva of some flies.

Tiger beetle head and mandibles

Southern black widow

Madagascan sunset moth

Pine processionary caterpillars

mandibles The jaws of an insect.

metamorphosis The process of changing form. Insects develop from young to adults either by simple or complete metamorphosis.

migration A group of animals traveling from one region to another, usually to breed or to find enough food to eat during winter or summer. Some butterflies travel thousands of miles as part of their annual migration, while some tiny beetles and springtails will migrate just a few inches to avoid cold soil temperatures.

mimicry A survival tool, with which an animal copies or imitates another animal. Insects and spiders are able to fool attackers into thinking they are dangerous or poisonous when they are not, and thus avoid being eaten.

molt The process of shedding an outer layer of the body. Insects and spiders molt their old exoskeletons so they can grow bigger.

nymph The young stage of insects that look similar to their parents and, through a series of molts, undergo simple metamorphosis to become adults.

ocelli Small, light-sensitive eyes. Many insects have three ocelli on the top of their head, which help flying insects stay level in flight, or tell insects that come out at night when it's getting dark.

order A large group of related plants or animals. Insects are divided into about 30 different orders, each with certain features in common. Spiders belong to only one order within the arachnids. An order is divided into smaller groups, from suborders, families, and genera, down to species.

ovipositor A tube at the tip of a female insect's abdomen used for laying eggs. The ovipositor of a wasp or bee has evolved into its stinger.

parasite A plant or animal that lives or feeds off another plant or animal, called a host. A parasitic insect will feed on the blood or body tissue of its living host, usually without killing the host but still making it very ill.

pedipalp A spider sense organ. A spider has two pedipalps, or palps—appendages at the front of its cephalothorax that it uses to touch, taste, and smell. A male spider also uses modified pedipalps to transfer sperm to the female during mating.

pheromone A chemical message or signal, used by many animals to communicate, usually with the same species—to attract a mate, find food, or warn others of danger.

predator An animal that hunts or preys on other animals for its food.

proboscis A tubelike mouthpart used by moths and butterflies to suck up liquid food.

pupa The stage in development that an insect undergoes to finish complete metamorphosis. Inside a tough pupal case, it changes dramatically as its juvenile body parts break down and adult features emerge.

scavenger An animal that feeds on food scraps or on rotting organic matter, such as corpses, dung, and shed skin.

simple metamorphosis One of two main ways in which an insect develops. The change is gradual, from an egg to a nymph to an adult. Grasshoppers, cockroaches, bugs, and dragonflies all go through this process of change to become an adult.

social insect An insect that lives with insects from the same species, caring for the young and finding food. Ants, termites, and some bees and wasps are social insects.

species A group of plants or animals that have certain features in common and usually breed only with one another.

spigots Tubes that spin spider silk into strands.

spinnerets Two to six fingerlike organs at the tip of a spider's abdomen. Various types of silk made by the spider emerge from the spinnerets.

spiracle A breathing hole in the side of an insect that takes oxygen into the body and expels waste gases, such as carbon dioxide. Insects have between two and eleven pairs of spiracles. Spiders may also have one to two pairs of these breathing holes.

stabilimenta Lines of thick silk in zigzag patterns. They protect and strengthen a spider's web.

swarm A mass of insects, such as bees or locusts, that collect or move around together for eating, mating, or finding a new nest site.

thorax The middle section of an insect's body. It is full of muscles that drive the insect's one to two pairs of wings and three pairs of legs, all of which are attached to it.

trachea A breathing tube. Humans and other vertebrates have only one trachea, which leads to the lungs. Insects and some spiders have a whole network of tracheae that carry oxygen to every organ and cell.

tympana Membranes that act like ears in crickets, grasshoppers, and cicadas. The tympana vibrate when they receive sounds, and this information is carried to the brain via the nervous system, so the insect can hear.

venom A chemical that is injected into another animal to kill or paralyze it or to deter it from attacking. The venom of spiders and some insects also helps liquify the prey so it can be sucked up.

vertebrate An animal that has a backbone, such as fishes, birds, reptiles, and mammals.

Jungle nymph

Grasshopper in flight

Index

The publishers would like to thank the following people for their assistance in the preparation of this book: Barbara Bakowski, James Clark, Renee Clark, and Lynn Strong.
Our special thanks to the following children who feature in the photographs: Sienna Berney, Irene Finkelde, Lewis Nicholson, Jeremy Sequeira, and Julian Sequeira.
PICTURE CREDITS (t=top, b=bottom, l=left, r=right, c=center, f=flap, F=Front, C=Cover, B=Back)
AdLibitum 5b, 8bl, 15cr, 17bc, 39bc, 51bl, 54t (M. Kaniewski). **Auscape** 61b (K. Atkinson), 18tl (J.Cancalosi), 42br (M. Doolittle-Peter Arnold),14cl, 49c, 56t (P. Goetgheluck-Pho.n.e), 11bc (C. A. Henley), 44cr (J. Shaw), 36cr (J. Sierra-OSF). **Bruce Coleman Ltd.** 20cl (J. Burton), 19br (R.P. Carr), 20tr, 35b, 61c (M. P. L. Fogden), 14tr, 26c (K.Taylor), 17tc (P . Zabransky). **CSIRO** 32bl (R. Moran/M. Robertson). **E.T. Archive** 58l (Private Collection, Naples). **Image Library-State Library of New South Wales** 36l. **Frank Lane Picture Agency** 54c (B. Borrell), 38tr (S.C. Brown), 48cr (Silvestris). **Minden Pictures** 24l (M. Moffett). **Nature Focus** 48bl (C. Bento), 53b (R. Mascord). **NHPA** 36tr (G. I. Bernard). **Oxford Scientific Films** 18tr (C.Bromhall), 34l (S. Camazine), 16l (M. Fogden), 54t (J. Mitchell), 58tr (S. Morris), 28tr (R.Packwood), 44tr (P. Parks), 57tl (V. Sinha). **The Photo Library** 23cr (P. Cheskey), 22c (Eye of Science/SPL), 22tr (R.R. Hansen), 12cr (C. Krebs), 39tc (Nuridsany & Perennou/SPL), 10bl, 50r (D. Scharf/SPL), 43b (R. Smith), 10bc, 10tr, 11bl (A. Syred/SPL), 9c (Dr, Paul Zahl). **Photo Researchers Inc.** 12ctr, 12tr (L. Lessin). **Planet Earth Pictures** 17c (G. du Feu), 52l, 57c, 59tr (S. Hopkin), 51tl (W.B. Irwin), 24tr, 35t, (D.P. Maitland), 52r (P. Palmer). **Premaphotos Wildlife** 29t, 40l, 43t, 44bl, 61t (K. G. Preston-Mafham). **Tom Stack and Associates** 32tr, 40r (D.M. Dennis), 26bl (J. Shaw).

ILLUSTRATION CREDITS
Susanna Addario 10tc. **Anne Bowman** 30cr, 34b, 35b, 35b, 60bc, 60t, 61b, 61r, 62bl. **Sandra Doyle/Wildlife Art** 4br, 5tr, 6tr, 7tl, 10/11c, 11c, 11tr, 18/19c, 18b, 18cl, 19b, 31tl, 38b, 38c, 38t, 39b, 39c, 39tr, 46cr, 46br, 47br, 47bc, 50b, 50t, 51b, 51c, 51tr, 52/53c, 52t, 53b, 53tr, 53tr, 62tr, 62br, 63br. **Simone End** 10bc, 11bl. **Christer Eriksson** 8tl, 28/29c. **Ray Grinaway** 6tl, 8/9c, 8r, 9cr, 9tr, 10tl, 28t, 28b, 29r, 29bc, 31br, 44/45c, 44t, 45r, 47tl, 54b, 54t, 55b, 55c. **Ian Jackson/Wildlife Art** 6cr, 6br, 12b, 12cl, 12ct, 12tl, 13b, 13c, 14/15c, 14b, 15b. **Frank Knight** 16br, 16tc, 16tl, 17bl, 17r. **David Kirshner** 8tc, 9bl. **Rob Mancini** 4tr, 7c, 22br, 22l, 23br, 23c, 26tl, 46tr, 47c, 48bl, 48t, 49b, 49c, 56c, 56t, 57b, 57cb, 57r, 63tl. **James McKinnon** 4crb, 31cl, 34/35c, 34r, 34tl, 42c, 42t, 43b, 43l, 43r, 43tr, 60c, 61l, 63bl. **Steve Roberts/Wildlife Art** 7r, 7cl, 20/21c, 21r, 21tl, 26/27c, 26bc, 26t, 27b, 27cr, 27t, 30tr, 31tr, 32bc, 32br, 32cl, 32t, 33r, 33c, 40b, 40t, 41b, 41c, 62tl, 63tr. **Trevor Ruth** 8bc. **Claudia Saraceni** 28b, 28t, 29b, 29r. **Chris Shields/Wildlife Art** 30br, 36b, 36c, 37b, 37c, 58bl, 58cl, 58t, 59b, 59c. **Kevin Stead** 4crt, 7cr, 7tr, 9br, 10bl, 11br, 11bc, 11cr, 14tl, 14tr, 16/17c, 16bl, 24/25c, 24b, 24cc, 24tl, 24tr, 25b, 60bl.

COVER CREDITS
Sandra Doyle/Wildlife Art Ffbr, FCtl, FCbc, FCcr, FCcrt, FCct, FCtr, BCcl, BCcrb, Bftr, Bfbr. **Ray Grinaway** Ffct. **Ian Jackson/Wildlife Art** FCtr, BCtc. **Rob Mancini** Ffcb, Ffbl, FCclt, FCcl, FCcrb, BCbc, BCtr, BCcr, Bfcl, Bfbl. **Steve Roberts/Wildlife Art** Fft, FCclb, FCbl, FCc, FCbr, BCtl, BCbl, BCcr, Bfbc. **Chris Shields/Wildlife Art** BCbr.